DATE NUT TORTE
June Hovland, Rochester, Minnesota
(PICTURED ON PAGE 8)

Whether I serve my torte with coffee at a luncheon or in the evening when friends visit, I always get compliments. My husband, three children and five grandchildren are all good eaters, and it's a joy to prepare this dessert for them, too!

>   2 eggs
>   1/2 cup sugar
>   1/2 cup packed brown sugar
>   2/3 cup all-purpose flour
>   1 teaspoon baking powder
>   1/4 teaspoon salt
>   1 cup chopped walnuts
>   1 cup chopped dates
> **Whipped cream**

In a mixing bowl, beat eggs. Gradually add sugars and beat until well mixed. Combine flour, baking powder and salt; add to mixing bowl and mix until moistened. Stir in nuts and dates. Pour into a greased 8-in. square baking pan. Bake at 350° for 30 minutes. Torte top will be crusty and the inside chewy. Cut into squares and serve with a dollop of whipped cream. **Yield:** 9 servings.

CHOCOLATE NOUGAT CAKE
Melody Sroufe, Wichita, Kansas

A wonderful lady who baby-sat me as a child gave me a recipe book of her handwritten specialties for a wedding gift. This one is my favorite.

>   1/3 cup margarine, softened
> 1-1/4 cups plus 2 tablespoons sugar, *divided*
>   2 eggs, *separated*
>   2 squares (1 ounce *each*) unsweetened
>   chocolate, melted
> 1-1/3 cups all-purpose flour
> 1-1/4 teaspoons baking powder
>   1/2 teaspoon salt
>   3/4 cup plus 2 tablespoons milk
>   1/2 cup finely chopped nuts
> **SEVEN-MINUTE FROSTING:**
> 1-1/2 cups sugar
>   1/3 cup cold water
>   2 egg whites, room temperature
>   1/4 teaspoon cream of tartar
>   1 teaspoon vanilla extract

In a large mixing bowl, cream margarine and 3/4 cup plus 2 tablespoons sugar until fluffy. Blend in egg yolks and chocolate. Sift together flour, baking powder and salt; add alternately with milk to creamed mixture. Stir in nuts. Beat egg whites with remaining sugar until stiff peaks form; fold gently into batter. Pour into two greased and floured 8-in. baking pans. Bake at 350° for 30-35 minutes.

Cool in pans on a rack for 10 minutes before removing from pans. Cool completely. For frosting, combine all ingredients except vanilla in the top of a double boiler. With an electric mixer, beat on low for 30 seconds. Cook over boiling water for 7 minutes, beating constantly on high until stiff peaks form. Remove from heat and add vanilla. Beat 2-3 minutes or until frosting has a spreading consistency. Frost cake. **Yield:** 12 servings.

HIMMEL FUTTER TORTE
Marsha Napientek, Franklin, Wisconsin
(PICTURED ON PAGE 9)

This recipe was a favorite of my grandma's. As kids, we called it "Dark Secret" because Grandma would vary the fruit with the season and we never knew what she hid under the cream!

>   4 eggs
>   2 cups sugar
>   2 tablespoons shortening, softened
>   1 teaspoon vanilla extract
>   1/2 cup all-purpose flour
>   2 teaspoons baking powder
>   1 teaspoon salt
> 2-1/2 cups chopped dates
>   1 cup chopped walnuts
>   2 oranges, peeled and sectioned
>   2 bananas, peeled and sliced
>   1 cup raspberries
>   1 can (8 ounces) pineapple chunks, drained
>   1 cup heavy cream, whipped

In a large mixing bowl, beat eggs and sugar until light. Add shortening and vanilla; beat well. Combine flour, baking powder, salt, dates and nuts; stir into mixing bowl and mix well. Spread in a greased 13-in. x 9-in. x 2-in. baking pan. Bake at 350° for 40-45 minutes or until cake tests done. Cool on a wire rack. Break torte into small pieces and arrange on a serving plate. Just before serving, place fruit on top and cover with whipped cream. Fruit can be varied by season. **Yield:** 12-15 servings.

BLACK WALNUT POUND CAKE
Betty Godfrey, Salisbury, North Carolina
(PICTURED ON PAGE 9)

I still remember my grandmother making this cake when I was a child...oh, how good it smelled and tasted!

>   1 cup butter, softened
>   1/2 cup shortening
>   3 cups sugar
>   5 eggs
>   3 cups all-purpose flour
>   1 teaspoon baking powder
>   1 cup whole milk
>   1 teaspoon vanilla extract
> 1/4 to 1/2 teaspoon almond extract
>   1 cup chopped black walnuts
> **CREAM CHEESE FROSTING:**
>   1 package (8 ounces) cream cheese, softened

GRANDMA'S
Great Desserts

❤ CONTENTS ❤

PICTURED ON OUR COVER. Clockwise from top left: Sour Cream Pound Cake (p. 20), Spiced Devil's Food Cake (p. 16), Old-Fashioned Strawberry Shortcake (p. 20), Apple Pie (p. 81), Fudge Brownies (p. 47) and Lemon Snowdrops (p. 59).

Cakes & Tortes

NOTHING shows off your baking skills better than a beautiful cake. And what better recipe to follow than one that's been carefully tested, perfected and passed down by a grandmother?

Grandma used simple ingredients she had on hand—flour, sugar, butter, eggs and fruit—to concoct perfect pound cakes, old-fashioned fruitcakes, tempting tortes, and a host of other cakes that have become family classics. Even during the Depression, when supplies were limited, her resourcefulness produced one of the most popular and delicious cakes: Eggless-Milkless-Butterless Cake!

Old-time grandmothers learned how to bake many of those moist, mouth-watering cakes by memory while watching *their* mothers and grandmothers bake —sometimes without the aid of a cookbook or written recipe! In fact, some family favorites have been lost because they were never written down.

Fortunately, we've recorded dozens of those time-honored, treasured cake recipes in this chapter for you and your family to enjoy. That way, you can have your grandma's cake...and eat it, too!

SKILLET PINEAPPLE UPSIDE-DOWN CAKE
Bernardine Melton, Paola, Kansas
(PICTURED ON PAGE 4)

For a change of pace, you can substitute fresh or frozen peach slices for the pineapple in this old-fashioned recipe.

- 1/2 cup butter
- 1 cup packed brown sugar
- 1 can (20 ounces) sliced pineapple
- 1/2 cup chopped pecans
- 3 eggs, room temperature, *separated*
- 1 cup sugar
- 1 teaspoon vanilla extract
- 1 cup all-purpose flour
- 1 teaspoon baking powder
- 1/4 teaspoon salt
- Maraschino cherries

Melt butter in a 9- or 10-in. cast-iron or other ovenproof skillet. Add brown sugar; mix well until sugar melts. Drain pineapple, reserving 1/3 cup juice. Arrange pineapple slices in a single layer over sugar (a few slices from can will not be used). Sprinkle pecans over pineapple; set aside. In a mixing bowl, beat egg yolks until thick and lemon-colored. Gradually add sugar, beating well. Blend in vanilla and reserved pineapple juice. Combine flour, baking powder and salt; add to batter. In another bowl, beat egg whites until stiff but not dry; fold into batter. Spoon into skillet. Bake at 375° for 30-35 minutes or until center of cake springs back when lightly touched. Allow to set 10 minutes before inverting onto serving plate. Place cherries in center of pineapple slices. **Yield:** 8-10 servings.

VANILLA WAFER COCONUT CAKE
Jane Muedeking, Tracy, Minnesota

This cake recipe, which came from my mother in Alabama, contains no flour—but it's delicious!

- 1 cup butter, softened
- 2 cups sugar
- 6 eggs
- 1 box (12 ounces) vanilla wafers, crushed
- 1/2 cup milk
- 1-1/2 cups flaked coconut
- 1 cup chopped pecans
- Whipped cream *or* ice cream, optional

In a large mixing bowl, cream butter and sugar. Add eggs, one at a time, beating well after each until light and fluffy. Add wafers alternately with milk. Fold in coconut and nuts. Pour into a greased and floured 10-in. tube pan (lined with brown paper if pan does not have a removable bottom). Bake at 350° for 1-1/4 hours, testing after 1 hour. Cool in pan on wire rack 15 minutes before removing to serving plate. Cool completely. If desired, top with whipped cream or ice cream. **Yield:** 12-16 servings.

CREAM CHEESE POUND CAKE
Betty Smith, Evans, Georgia

Warm a slice of this cake in the microwave for about 25 seconds. Then serve it with a scoop of butter-pecan ice cream, fresh fruit, or alone!

- 1-1/2 cups butter *or* margarine, softened
- 3 cups sugar
- 1 package (8 ounces) cream cheese, softened
- 6 eggs
- 3 cups all-purpose flour
- 1/2 teaspoon baking powder

In a large mixing bowl, cream butter, sugar and cream cheese. Add eggs, one at a time, beating well after each addition. Add flour and baking powder; mix well. Pour into a greased and floured 10-in. tube pan. Bake at 325° for about 1 hour and 30 minutes or until cake tests done. Cool in pan 10 minutes before removing. Cake ages and freezes well. **Yield:** 12-16 servings.

HELP YOURSELF. Opposite page, top to bottom: Poppy Seed Torte (p. 6), Prune Cake (p. 6), Skillet Pineapple Upside-Down Cake (above).

LEMON CURD
Noreen McGaffee, Orland, California

This recipe was my great-grandmother's, but she never measured anything. Fortunately, Mom watched her over the years and finally came up with the measurements.

3/4 cup fresh lemon juice (about 4 lemons)
Finely grated peel of 4 lemons
    4 eggs, beaten
    2 cups sugar
    1/2 cup butter *or* margarine

Combine all ingredients in a large saucepan. Bring to a boil over medium heat, stirring constantly. Boil and stir for 2 minutes. Pour into jars; cool. Store in refrigerator or freezer. Sauce is good on pound cake, muffins, pancakes and waffles. **Yield:** 3 cups.

FROSTING FINESSE: Before frosting a cake, place strips of waxed paper on the serving plate under the bottom cake layer. After frosting, carefully remove the waxed paper—you'll have a clean plate.

• Unfrosted cake layers can be frozen on a cookie sheet until firm, wrapped separately with plastic wrap and kept in the freezer. When they're ready for use, just thaw, frost and serve.

PRUNE CAKE
Laura Olson, Mesa, Arizona
(PICTURED ON PAGE 4)

This cake recipe was given to me years ago by a friend, who got it from her mother. I'm 82 years old, have been married 57 years and still enjoy baking this cake for my husband.

1-1/2 cups sugar
    2 cups all-purpose flour
    1 teaspoon baking soda
    1 teaspoon ground nutmeg
    1 teaspoon ground cinnamon
    1 teaspoon salt
    1 cup vegetable oil
    3 eggs, beaten
    1/2 cup buttermilk
    1 teaspoon vanilla extract
    1 cup cut-up prunes, cooked
    1 cup chopped nuts
TOPPING:
    1/2 cup butter *or* margarine
    1/3 cup buttermilk
    1 teaspoon vanilla extract
    1/2 teaspoon baking soda
    3/4 cup sugar

In a large mixing bowl, combine first six ingredients. Add oil, eggs, buttermilk and vanilla; mix well. Fold in prunes and nuts. Pour into an ungreased 13-in. x 9-in. x 2-in. baking pan. Bake at 350° for 45 minutes. Meanwhile, combine all topping ingredients in a saucepan. Bring to a boil and boil 2 minutes. Pour over hot cake. Leave in pan to cool. **Yield:** 12-16 servings.

POPPY SEED TORTE
Corinne Haugstad, Hallock, Minnesota
(PICTURED ON PAGE 4)

I've loved this torte since I was a youngster, and now I can pass it on to my eight grandchildren. It's easy to make and tastes so good!

1/3 cup poppy seeds
    3/4 cup milk
1-1/2 teaspoons vanilla extract
    3/4 cup butter *or* margarine, softened
1-1/2 cups sugar
    2 cups cake flour
2-1/2 teaspoons baking powder
    1/4 teaspoon salt
    4 egg whites, stiffly beaten
FILLING:
    3/4 cup sugar
    5 teaspoons cornstarch
2-1/4 cups milk
    6 egg yolks, lightly beaten
    1 teaspoon vanilla extract
    1/4 cup chopped walnuts, optional
Confectioners' sugar

Place poppy seeds and milk in a small bowl; soak for 1 hour. Add vanilla. In a large mixing bowl, cream butter and sugar until fluffy. Add poppy seed mixture. Sift together flour, baking powder and salt; add to creamed mixture. Fold in egg whites. Spread into two well-greased and lightly floured 8-in. round baking pans. Bake at 375° for 20-25 minutes or until cakes test done. Cool 5 minutes before removing from pans. Cool thoroughly. For filling, combine sugar, cornstarch, milk and egg yolks in a saucepan; cook until thickened and bubbly. Add vanilla, and nuts if desired. Split cakes in half and spread filling between layers. Chill. Before serving, dust top with confectioners' sugar. **Yield:** 10-14 servings.

BEFORE YOU BEGIN BAKING, KEEP IN MIND:

• When a recipe in this cookbook calls for an egg, it is referring to a *large* egg.

• When a recipe lists only butter and not margarine, it's important to use real butter. Butterlike substitutes and "light butters" may be whipped with water or other ingredients, which can affect baking results.

• To accurately measure dry ingredients, use sets of measuring cups which can be leveled off and come in 1/4-, 1/3-, 1/2- and 1-cup sizes. For measuring liquids, use the clear 1-, 2- or 4-cup size with subdivisions marked on the side of the cup. Be sure to set the cup on a flat surface and measure from eye level.

• Sweetened condensed milk and evaporated milk are two different products and *cannot* be used interchangeably in recipes.

Sweetened condensed milk has a thicker consistency and is great for desserts because it will not get "sugary" when heated and will not form ice crystals in frozen desserts. Also, it thickens without heat when combined with an acidic juice, such as lemon, orange, pineapple or apple.

FROM GRANDMA'S KITCHEN:
Holiday Pound Cake

Nancy Reichert

"My grandmother was a great cook and a special lady. My desire is to live to be remembered as the hospitable lady she was."

Snow rarely falls in Thomasville, Georgia, but when the Christmas season begins, Nancy Reichert enjoys cooking up a storm for her family and three young granddaughters—including a special holiday cake that reminds her of her own grandmother.

"I learned most everything about cooking from my grandmother, who was a super Southern cook," says Nancy, whose own mother died when she was young. "My fondest memories are of the times I spent cooking with my grandmother, who we affectionately called 'Mom'. She had eight children and lived on a farm and would spread that old dinner table with country ham, grits, homemade biscuits, jams and jellies, loads of vegetables and delicious desserts!

"Although this Holiday Pound Cake recipe didn't come from my grandmother, I think of her when I make it—it's the kind of dessert she often made," Nancy explains.

The recipe came from a teacher who brought the cake to a Christmas party at an elementary school where Nancy worked several years ago. Nancy sampled a piece, wrote down the recipe, and has made the cake for parties and as gifts every year since.

"This cake is attractive and it tastes good, too. To add a festive touch, I glaze the top and decorate it

with pecans from my trees in the backyard, plus red and green cherries to look like poinsettias," Nancy says.

Now her Holiday Pound Cake makes an annual appearance at the Christmas party of the local vocational high school where Nancy's been secretary for 11 years. She always gets requests for the recipe, and since everyone brings a dessert, Nancy enjoys swapping recipes.

"Down here in south Georgia, we still do it like Grandma did in her day...we cook in abundance and we swap recipes," Nancy explains, adding, "Swapping recipes is almost as much fun as sampling the desserts!"

As secretary, Nancy voluntarily types up the recipes on sheets and hands out copies to the teachers the day after the party.

Nancy's recipe-swapping has resulted in loads of dessert recipes, which suits her sweet-loving husband just fine. And just as her grandmother instilled in her an interest in baking, Nancy hopes to inspire her own preschool-age granddaughters (who visit nearly every weekend) to one day make desserts like Holiday Pound Cake. For now, though, Nancy is taking it one step at a time. "They're still pretty young, so I'm teaching them to make mud pies first," she says with a laugh.

HOLIDAY POUND CAKE

    1 cup butter, softened
    1 package (8 ounces) cream cheese,
      softened
1-1/2 cups sugar
    4 eggs
1-1/2 teaspoons vanilla extract
2-1/4 cups cake flour
1-1/2 teaspoons baking powder
    1/2 teaspoon salt
    3/4 cup well-drained maraschino
      cherries
    1 cup chopped pecans, *divided*
1-1/2 cups confectioners' sugar
    2 to 3 tablespoons milk
Additional cherries and pecans for garnish, optional

In a large mixing bowl, cream butter, cream cheese and sugar. Add eggs, one at a time, beating well after each addition. Add vanilla. Sift flour together with baking powder and salt; stir into creamed mixture. Fold in cherries and 1/2 cup nuts. Sprinkle remaining nuts into a greased 10-in. fluted tube pan. Pour batter into pan. Bake at 325° for about 70 minutes or until cake tests done. Cool cake in pan 5 minutes on wire rack before removing from pan. Cool thoroughly. Make a glaze with confectioners' sugar and milk; drizzle over cake. Garnish top with cherries and pecans if desired. **Yield:** 12-16 servings.

ACTIVE INGREDIENT: Wet and dry ingredients for cakes can be mixed separately ahead of time, but once the baking powder or soda is wet, it starts to activate, and the batter should be put in the oven promptly.

OLD TIMES NOT FORGOTTEN. Clockwise from bottom left: Date Nut Torte (p. 10), Forgotten Torte (p. 11), Himmel Futter Torte (p. 10), Black Walnut Pound Cake (p. 10), Aunt Murna's Jam Cake (p. 11).

1/4 cup butter, softened
1 box (16 ounces) confectioners' sugar
1 teaspoon vanilla extract

In a large mixing bowl, cream butter, shortening and sugar. Add eggs, one at a time, beating well after each addition. Sift together flour and baking powder; add alternately with milk and extracts to creamed mixture, beating on low speed just until combined. Fold in nuts. Pour into a greased and floured 10-in. tube pan. Bake at 325° for about 1 hour and 25 minutes or until cake tests done. Cool 10 minutes on a wire rack before removing from pan. Cool thoroughly. For frosting, beat cream cheese and butter in a medium mixing bowl. Add sugar and mix well. Add vanilla; beat until smooth. Spread on cooled cake. Cake can be made with or without frosting. **Yield:** 12-16 servings.

HARD SAUCE FOR CAKE
Deb Brass, Cedar Falls, Iowa

My grandmother often dressed up leftover plain cake with this sauce. It also goes well with gingerbread. For fun, I love to page through my great-grandmother's old cookbooks.

1 cup sugar
2 tablespoons cornstarch
1/2 teaspoon salt
2 cups boiling water
1/2 teaspoon vanilla extract
1/4 cup butter

Combine sugar, cornstarch and salt in a saucepan. Gradually stir in water; bring to a boil. Cook and stir for 15 minutes until smooth, thickened and clear. Remove from heat; stir in vanilla and butter. Serve hot over cake. **Yield:** 1 cup.

AUNT MURNA'S JAM CAKE
Mrs. Eddie Robinson, Lawrenceburg, Kentucky
(PICTURED ON PAGE 9)

I remember Aunt Murna telling me that she created her Jam Cake recipe as a very young girl. Through the years she made improvements, such as soaking the raisins in crushed pineapple. This cake is a favorite at our annual family reunions and at Christmastime.

1 cup raisins
1 can (8 ounces) crushed pineapple with juice
1 cup butter, softened
4 eggs
1 jar (12 ounces) blackberry jam *or* 1 cup homemade blackberry jam
2/3 cup buttermilk
2-1/2 cups all-purpose flour
1 cup sugar
1/3 cup unsweetened cocoa
1 teaspoon baking soda
1 teaspoon ground cinnamon
1 teaspoon ground nutmeg
1/2 teaspoon ground cloves
1 cup chopped pecans

CARAMEL ICING:
1 cup butter
2 cups packed brown sugar
1/2 cup milk
3-1/2 to 4 cups sifted confectioners' sugar

Soak raisins in pineapple and juice several hours or overnight. In a large mixing bowl, cream butter. Add eggs, one at a time, beating well after each addition. Add jam and buttermilk; beat until well blended. Sift together dry ingredients; add to batter. Beat on low just until ingredients are combined. Stir in raisins, pineapple and pecans. Pour into two greased and floured 9-in. round cake pans. Bake at 350° for 50 minutes or until cakes test done. Cool in pans 10 minutes on a wire rack before removing to rack. For icing, melt butter in a saucepan over medium heat. Stir in brown sugar and milk; bring to a boil. Remove from heat. Cool just until warm; beat in enough confectioners' sugar until icing is of spreading consistency. Add more sugar for thicker icing; more milk to thin it. Frost cooled cake. **Yield:** 12-16 servings.

FORGOTTEN TORTE
Frances McFarlane, Winnipeg, Manitoba
(PICTURED ON PAGE 8)

This torte is "forgotten" in the oven overnight, but we never forget how good it tastes when we eat it!

6 egg whites, room temperature
1/2 teaspoon cream of tartar
1/4 teaspoon salt
1-1/2 cups sugar
1 teaspoon vanilla extract
1/8 teaspoon almond extract
1 cup heavy cream
Red food coloring, optional
Raspberries *or* strawberries

In a large mixing bowl, beat egg whites, cream of tartar and salt at medium speed until foamy. Add sugar a little at a time, beating well. Add extracts. Continue beating until stiff glossy peaks form. Grease the bottom only of a 9-in. tube pan with removable bottom. Spread batter evenly in pan. Place in a preheated 450° oven and immediately turn off heat. Let stand in oven overnight. The next day, loosen edges of torte with a sharp knife and turn onto serving platter. Just before serving, whip cream until stiff; tint with food coloring if desired. Frost with cream and top with berries. **Yield:** 10-12 servings.

> **CLEVER CAKE TIPS:** For a moister cake, place a small bowl of water in the oven while the cake bakes.
> • For best results, bake cakes in center of oven, and don't open the oven door until it is almost done.
> • If a cake is difficult to remove from the pan, return it to a warm oven for 30-60 seconds. Then invert it onto a serving plate or cooling rack.
> • Let cakes cool completely before icing or frosting (unless directions specify otherwise).
> • Use a wet knife to slice sticky, moist cakes and cheesecakes. (Keep a tall glass of hot water handy and dip the knife before cutting. Wipe knife with a paper towel after each cut.)

LEMON TORTE
Kristi Twohig, Oshkosh, Wisconsin

This beautiful, light treat has an easy-to-make meringue base that's complemented with tart and sweet fillings.

>   4 eggs, *separated*
> 1/4 teaspoon cream of tartar
> 1-1/2 cups sugar, *divided*
>   1 teaspoon vanilla extract
>   2 tablespoons lemon juice
>   2 tablespoons grated lemon peel
>   1 pint whipping cream, whipped, *divided*

In a mixing bowl, beat egg whites and cream of tartar until stiff and glossy. Gradually beat in 1 cup sugar. Add vanilla. Spread in a well-greased 13-in. x 9-in. x 2-in. baking pan. Bake at 300° for 1 hour. Remove to a draft-free spot to cool. Meanwhile, in the top of a double boiler, beat egg yolks until lemon-colored. Add remaining sugar, lemon juice and peel. Cook over hot but not boiling water, stirring occasionally, until thick. Cool thoroughly. Spread half of cream over meringue shell; cover with custard. Spread remaining cream on top. Cover and refrigerate. Torte is best made a day ahead. **Yield:** 16 servings.

OUT OF BAKING CHOCOLATE? For each square needed, substitute 1 square unsweetened chocolate along with 3 tablespoons unsweetened cocoa and 1 tablespoon shortening.

ORANGE DATE CAKE
Joyce Lewis, Lindsay, California

When it's time for dessert, this rich cake with orange syrup is a special treat for our farm family.

>   4 cups all-purpose flour
>   2 teaspoons baking soda
>   1 teaspoon salt
> 1-1/2 cups chopped dates
>   1 cup chopped walnuts
>   1 cup butter-flavored shortening
>   2 cups sugar
>   4 eggs
> Grated peel of 1 orange
>   2 cups buttermilk
> **ORANGE SYRUP:**
> Juice of 1 orange
>   1/2 to 3/4 cup sugar

Sift together flour, baking soda and salt; combine 1 cup with dates and walnuts. Set both mixtures aside. In a large mixing bowl, cream shortening and sugar until light and fluffy. Add eggs, one at a time, beating well after each addition. Add peel. Add flour mixtures. Stir in buttermilk just until blended. Spoon into a greased and floured 10-in. tube pan. Bake at 300° for 1-1/2 to 1-3/4 hours. Meanwhile, for syrup, heat orange juice and sugar in saucepan until sugar dissolves. Let stand 30 minutes. Cool cake 10 minutes in pan before removing. Cool 10 minutes more before pouring syrup over cake. **Yield:** 16-20 servings.

SPICE CAKE
Linda Peffer, Denison, Iowa

My Grandma Susie would take this wonderful cake to barn raisings and to barn dances, where my Grandpa Ward would also take his fiddle. I hope my two grandchildren will have such warm memories of me when they are grandparents.

> 1/2 cup butter, softened
>   2 cups packed dark brown sugar
>   1 cup buttermilk
>   2 eggs
>   2 cups all-purpose flour
>   1 teaspoon baking soda
>   2 teaspoons ground cinnamon
> 1/2 teaspoon ground cloves
> 1/2 teaspoon ground nutmeg
> **SEVEN-MINUTE FROSTING:**
>   2 unbeaten egg whites
> 1/4 teaspoon salt
>   2 teaspoons corn syrup
> 1-1/2 cups sugar
>   1/3 cup cold water
>   1 teaspoon vanilla extract

In a large mixing bowl, cream butter and sugar. Combine buttermilk and eggs; set aside. Combine dry ingredients; add alternately with buttermilk/eggs to creamed mixture. Pour into two greased 9-in. round baking pans. Bake at 350° for 25-30 minutes. For frosting, combine egg whites, salt, corn syrup, sugar and water in top of a double boiler. Beat with an electric mixer for 1 minute. Place over boiling water; beat constantly for 7 minutes, stopping only to scrape sides of pan. Remove from heat. Add vanilla; beat 1 more minute. Frost one cake layer; top with second layer and frost entire cake. Do not seal cake tightly when storing. **Yield:** 12 servings.

MAPLE NUT ANGEL FOOD CAKE
Doris Fett, Lake Lillian, Minnesota

This cake has been a favorite in our family for many years. It was a regular request when our three sons were young.

> 1-1/4 cups cake flour
>   3/4 cup packed brown sugar
> 1-1/2 cups egg whites
>   1/4 teaspoon salt
> 1-1/2 teaspoons cream of tartar
>   1 teaspoon vanilla extract
>   1/4 teaspoon maple flavoring
>   1 cup sugar
>   3/4 cup walnuts, finely chopped

Sift together flour and brown sugar; set aside. In a large mixing bowl, beat egg whites, salt and cream of tartar until soft peaks form. Add vanilla and maple flavoring. Add sugar a little at a time, beating until stiff. Gradually fold in flour/sugar mixture, about 1/4 at a time. Spoon half the batter into an ungreased angel food cake pan; sprinkle with nuts. Cut through batter with knife; spoon in remaining batter. Bake at 375° for about 35 minutes. Cool inverted on a wire rack. **Yield:** 12-16 servings.

FROM GRANDMA'S KITCHEN:
Rhubarb Squares

Ruth Windle

"My grandmother rarely used a cookbook, but her desserts always tasted delicious."

When the rhubarb stalks growing behind Ruth Windle's house in Kettle Falls, Washington turn a pinkish-red, it's not long before she has a batch of Rhubarb Squares baking in the oven. The sweet aroma reminds her of childhood days when she helped pick rhubarb from her grandmother's garden in Manitoba for that same delicious dessert.

Ruth enjoyed helping in the kitchen, whether it was at her grandma's house or on her parents' grain farm. Each Saturday after morning chores, Ruth and her three sisters would gather in the farm kitchen to help bake breads, buns, pies and desserts. Their "help" was appreciated, even if it often meant taking turns licking the spoon and sampling the batter!

"Mom used to teach us girls to bake different things each week, but, of course, only half of the cookie dough ever got baked," Ruth jokes.

Both her grandmother and her mother made Rhubarb Squares for family gatherings and special church functions, but the recipe wasn't written down. In fact, Ruth rarely saw them consult a cookbook for any recipe. "Both sides of my family are Mennonite, and most of the cooking was done from memory," she says.

The rhubarb recipe was passed around at churches and potlucks, though, and eventually found its way into a Mennonite cookbook that was compiled by ac-

quaintances of the family. Ruth received the cookbook from her mother as a gift and has carried on the tradition of making Rhubarb Squares for her family and church potlucks ever since...but these days, she shares the squares as a pastor's wife!

"I get many opportunities to entertain and cook for church functions, and this dessert always goes quickly," Ruth says. "I've received many compliments on what a great way it is to use rhubarb.

"One woman from church gives me extra rhubarb every summer, and what I don't use, I cut up and freeze for winter baking."

Outside the kitchen, Ruth sews children's clothes for her two young sons and daughter and for a local consignment shop. She also enjoys cross-stitch, teaches Sunday School and gives piano lessons at their home. "Our young children enjoy the kids I teach in our home and love Sunday School—even if Mommy is their teacher," says Ruth with a laugh, "especially when I bring along a plateful of Rhubarb Squares."

RHUBARB SQUARES

1-1/2 cups all-purpose flour
   3 tablespoons sugar
   3/4 cup butter
FILLING:
   3 tablespoons all-purpose flour
   3/4 cup cream
   2 cups sugar, *divided*
   4 eggs, *separated*
   2 teaspoons vanilla extract
   5 cups diced rhubarb

Combine flour and sugar; cut in butter until crumbly. Press into the bottom of a 13-in. x 9-in. x 2-in. baking pan. Bake at 350° for 10 minutes. Cool slightly. For filling, blend flour and cream in a mixing bowl until smooth. Add 1-1/4 cups sugar and egg yolks; mix well. Fold in vanilla and rhubarb. Pour into crust. Bake at 325° for 55-60 minutes or until a sharp knife inserted near center comes out clean. Meanwhile, make a meringue by beating egg whites until stiff. Add remaining sugar and beat again until stiff peaks form. Remove cake from oven; top with meringue immediately and broil lightly. **Yield:** 20-24 servings.

*T*hank God for dirty dishes
They have a tale to tell.
While other folks go hungry,
We're eating very well.
With home and health and happiness,
We surely shouldn't fuss,
For by this stack of evidence,
God's been good to us!

MOIST CHOCOLATE CAKE
Patricia Kreitz, Richland, Pennsylvania
(PICTURED ON PAGE 14)

This dark, moist cake is a birthday favorite. We love its tender texture and superb taste.

> **2 cups all-purpose flour**
> **1 teaspoon salt**
> **1 teaspoon baking powder**
> **2 teaspoons baking soda**
> **3/4 cup unsweetened cocoa**
> **2 cups sugar**
> **1 cup vegetable oil**
> **1 cup hot coffee**
> **1 cup milk**
> **2 eggs**
> **1 teaspoon vanilla extract**

FAVORITE ICING:
> **1 cup milk**
> **5 tablespoons all-purpose flour**
> **1/2 cup butter, softened**
> **1/2 cup shortening**
> **1 cup sugar**
> **1 teaspoon vanilla extract**

Sift together all dry ingredients in a large mixing bowl. Add oil, coffee and milk; mix at medium speed for 2 minutes. Add eggs and vanilla; beat 2 more minutes. Pour into two greased and floured 9-in. cake pans (or two 8-in. cake pans and six muffin cups). Bake at 325° for 25-30 minutes. Meanwhile, for icing, combine milk and flour in a saucepan; cook until thick. Cover and refrigerate. In a medium mixing bowl, beat butter, shortening, sugar and vanilla until creamy. Add chilled milk/flour mixture; beat for 10 minutes. Frost cooled cake. **Yield:** 12 servings.

BANANA PECAN CAKE
Bonnie L. Breja, Elberon, Iowa

This banana cake, topped with pecans and coconut, combines just the right amount of fruit and crunch.

> **1-1/2 cups sugar**
> **3/4 cup shortening**
> **2 eggs**
> **1 cup mashed bananas**
> **1 teaspoon vanilla extract**
> **2 cups cake flour**
> **1 teaspoon baking powder**
> **1 teaspoon baking soda**
> **1/2 teaspoon salt**
> **1/2 cup buttermilk**
> **1/2 cup chopped pecans**
> **1 cup flaked coconut**

PECAN FILLING:
> **1/2 cup sugar**
> **2 tablespoons all-purpose flour**
> **1/2 cup light cream**
> **2 tablespoons butter**

> PARTY FAVORITE. On opposite page: Moist Chocolate Cake (recipe above).

> **1/2 cup chopped pecans**
> **1/4 teaspoon salt**
> **1 teaspoon vanilla extract**

FLUFFY FROSTING:
> **1 egg white**
> **1/4 cup shortening**
> **1/4 cup butter, softened**
> **1 teaspoon vanilla extract**
> **2 cups confectioners' sugar**

In a large mixing bowl, cream sugar and shortening. Add eggs, one at a time, beating well after each addition. Blend in bananas and vanilla. Sift flour; then sift together with baking powder, soda and salt. Add alternately with buttermilk to the creamed mixture. Stir in nuts. Pour into two greased and floured 9-in. round cake pans. Sprinkle coconut on top of each cake. Bake at 375° for 25-30 minutes or until cakes test done. Cool in pans 10 minutes; remove and cool completely. For filling, combine sugar, flour, cream and butter in a saucepan. Cook over medium heat until thick. Add nuts, salt and vanilla; cool. Spread filling on one cake layer with coconut side up. Place second layer, coconut side up, on top. For frosting, beat egg white, shortening, butter and vanilla until smooth and creamy. Add sugar and beat until light and fluffy. Frost sides of cake only. If desired, cake can be made without frosting. **Yield:** 12 servings.

EGGNOG POUND CAKE
Audrey Kaalaas, Kirkland, Illinois

When you're having company, this cake—served with a custard sauce and a dash of nutmeg—inspires "oohs" and "aahs".

> **1 package (18-1/4 ounces) yellow cake mix**
> **1-1/4 cups nonalcoholic eggnog**
> **3 eggs**
> **1/4 cup butter, softened**
> **2 teaspoons ground nutmeg**
> **1/2 to 1 teaspoon vanilla extract**

CREAMY CUSTARD SAUCE:
> **1/4 cup sugar**
> **1 tablespoon cornstarch**
> **1/4 teaspoon salt**
> **1 cup milk**
> **1 egg yolk**
> **1/4 teaspoon vanilla extract**
> **1 teaspoon butter**
> **1/2 cup whipping cream, whipped**

Additional ground nutmeg, optional

In a large mixing bowl, combine first six ingredients. Beat on low until moistened. Increase speed to medium and beat 2 minutes. Pour into a greased and floured fluted tube pan. Bake at 350° for 40-45 minutes. Cool 10 minutes; invert on a wire rack. Meanwhile, for sauce, combine sugar, cornstarch and salt in a medium saucepan. Gradually stir in milk. Cook over medium heat until mixture thickens and boils, stirring constantly. Cook 1 minute. Remove from the heat. Beat egg yolk in a small bowl; stir in half of hot mixture, then return to saucepan and cook 1 minute on low. Remove from heat; stir in vanilla and butter. Cool completely. Fold in whipped cream; refrigerate. Serve sauce over cake slices; sprinkle nutmeg on top if desired. **Yield:** 20 servings.

SPICED DEVIL'S FOOD CAKE
Linda Yeamans, Ashland, Oregon
(PICTURED ON OUR COVER)

One of my mom's friends gave her this recipe when I was a child and it has been a family favorite ever since. When your "chocolate sweet tooth" acts up, this really hits the spot!

      1 cup butter, softened
      2 cups sugar
      4 eggs
      1 teaspoon vanilla extract
      2 cups all-purpose flour
      4 tablespoons unsweetened cocoa
      1 teaspoon baking powder
      1 teaspoon baking soda
      1 teaspoon ground cinnamon
   1/2 to 1 teaspoon ground nutmeg
   1/4 to 1/2 teaspoon ground cloves
      1 cup buttermilk
MOCHA ICING:
      1 box (16 ounces) confectioners' sugar
      4 tablespoons unsweetened cocoa
      6 tablespoons strong coffee
      6 tablespoons butter, melted
      1 teaspoon vanilla extract
Whole almonds, optional

In a large mixing bowl, cream butter and sugar. Add eggs, one at a time, beating well after each addition. Add vanilla. Sift together all dry ingredients; add alternately with buttermilk to creamed mixture. Pour into two greased and floured 9-in. cake pans. Bake at 350° for 30-35 minutes or until cakes test done. Cool. For icing, mix all ingredients except nuts until smooth. Frost one cake layer; top with second layer and frost entire cake. Garnish with almonds if desired. **Yield:** 12 servings.

⚘❤♥♥⚘

APPLESAUCE CAKE ROLL
Mozilla Jeno, Mount Carmel, Tennessee

This old-fashioned roll is pretty for parties and great for gifts, but it's also a real treat for a coffee break.

      4 eggs
      1 cup all-purpose flour
   1/2 teaspoon ground cinnamon
   1/4 teaspoon ground cloves
   3/4 cup sugar
   1/2 cup applesauce
FILLING:
      1 package (8 ounces) cream cheese, softened
      3 tablespoons milk
   1/4 cup confectioners' sugar
   1/2 cup raisins
Additional confectioners' sugar, optional

In a mixing bowl, beat eggs. Combine flour, cinnamon and cloves. Add to eggs along with sugar; mix well. Add apple-

sauce. Line a 15-in. x 10-in. x 1-in. pan with waxed paper, and grease and flour the paper. Pour batter into pan. Bake at 400° for 15 minutes. Turn out onto a linen towel dusted with confectioners' sugar. Peel off paper and roll cake up in towel. Let cool. Meanwhile, for filling, beat cream cheese, milk and sugar in a small mixing bowl. Stir in raisins. Unroll cake; spread filling to within 1 in. of edges. Roll up again. Dust with confectioners' sugar if desired. Refrigerate until serving time. Cut into 1-in. slices. **Yield:** 10 servings.

⚘❤♥♥⚘

POPPY SEED BUNDT CAKE
Dana Koss, Tofield, Alberta

This recipe, passed down from my mother, is perfect for church or social functions. It can be made ahead (it freezes beautifully) and is not sticky or crumbly—that's important if you're trying to walk around and socialize.

      6 tablespoons poppy seeds
      1 cup buttermilk
      1 cup butter *or* margarine, softened
   1-1/2 cups sugar
      4 eggs, *separated*
   2-1/2 cups all-purpose flour
      2 teaspoons baking powder
      1 teaspoon baking soda
   1/2 teaspoon salt
FILLING:
   1/3 cup sugar
      2 teaspoons unsweetened cocoa
      1 teaspoon ground cinnamon

Place poppy seeds and buttermilk in a bowl; soak for 2 hours. In a large mixing bowl, cream butter until fluffy. Add sugar and egg yolks; beat well. Combine remaining dry ingredients; add alternately with poppy seeds/buttermilk to creamed mixture. In another bowl, beat egg whites until stiff. Fold into batter; set aside. Combine filling ingredients; sprinkle one-third into bottom of a greased and floured 10-in. bundt pan. Pour in half of batter; "swirl" in half of remaining filling. Add remaining batter and filling, again swirling together. Bake at 350° for 1 hour. Turn out immediately onto wire rack to cool. **Yield:** 16-20 servings.

▼▼▼▼▼▼▼▼▼▼▼▼▼▼▼▼▼▼▼▼▼▼▼▼▼▼▼▼▼▼

*I baked this special chocolate cake—
It's just as light as a feather.
So I must be quite careful when
Transporting it in windy weather!*

⚘❤♥♥⚘

CHOCOLATE HOLIDAY CAKE
Mrs. John Gallahue, Piper City, Illinois

Don't let the length and steps of this recipe scare you. It's simple...and the fudgy richness will bring rave reviews from everyone.

CAKE:
   1/2 cup butter
   1/2 cup vegetable oil

Birthday Cake Had Secret Ingredient!

I remember when food staples like eggs and sugar were rationed. Our family of four could get six eggs a week at the local market. I really had to stretch those eggs to make them last a whole week!

Both of our sons have their birthdays 2 days apart in February, and I was determined to make them a birthday cake even during those rationing times. I only had one egg left and enough flour to make a single-layer cake with a little extra sugar for icing.

Wouldn't you know it…the cake fell in the middle! Not to worry. I cut the cake in half, iced the bottom half, put a slice of bread in the hollow between the layers and slapped enough chocolate icing over the bread and back side that no one ever knew the difference! —*Louise P. Vaccaro, Hemet, California*

        3 squares (1 ounce *each*) unsweetened chocolate
        1 cup water
        2 cups all-purpose flour
        1 teaspoon baking soda
        2 cups sugar
        2 eggs, beaten
    1/2 cup sour milk*
        1 teaspoon vanilla extract
FILLING:
        1 can (5 ounces) evaporated milk
    3/4 cup sugar
    1/4 cup water
    1/4 cup chopped seedless raisins
    1/2 cup chopped dates
        1 teaspoon vanilla extract
    1/2 cup chopped pecans
CHOCOLATE ICING:
        1 package (6 ounces) semisweet chocolate chips
    1/2 cup sour cream
Dash salt
Whipped cream, optional

In a small saucepan, combine butter, oil and chocolate. Cook over low heat, stirring until chocolate melts. Add water; cool 15 minutes. In another bowl, combine remaining cake ingredients and beat well. (*To sour milk, add 1-1/2 teaspoons vinegar to milk; let stand 5 minutes.) Fold chocolate mixture into batter. Pour into two greased and floured 8-in. cake pans. Bake at 350° for 30-35 minutes or until cakes test done. Cool in pans 5 minutes. Meanwhile, for filling, combine milk, sugar and water in a small saucepan. Cook over medium heat, stirring to dissolve sugar. Add raisins and dates. Cook until thickened, stirring constantly, about 5 minutes. Remove from heat; add vanilla and nuts. Cool. For frosting, melt chips in top of a double boiler over hot water. Remove from heat. Stir in sour cream and salt; beat with a spoon until smooth. Cool 5 minutes or until frosting is of spreading consistency. Place one cake layer, upside down, on a plate. Spread filling on top and place other layer over. Frost entire cake. Chill 1 hour before serving. Serve with a dollop of whipped cream if desired. **Yield:** 12 servings.

COFFEE NUT TORTE
Ruth Ann Stelfox, Raymond, Alberta

Every year at Bible school when I was growing up, we enjoyed this dessert as an extra-special treat. I still serve it to appreciative guests.

    1/2 cup butter *or* margarine
        1 cup sugar
        3 eggs, *separated*
    1/2 cup all-purpose flour
        2 teaspoons baking powder
        2 cups fine graham cracker crumbs
        1 cup cold strong coffee
        1 teaspoon vanilla extract
    3/4 cup chopped nuts
FILLING:
        1 package (3.4 ounces) instant vanilla pudding
            mix
1-1/4 cups whole milk
        1 teaspoon instant coffee granules
    1/2 cup heavy cream, whipped

In a large mixing bowl, cream butter and sugar. Add egg yolks; beat until light. Sift together flour and baking powder; add crumbs. Add alternately with coffee to creamed mixture, beating well until smooth. Stir in vanilla and nuts. In another bowl, beat egg whites until stiff; fold into batter. Pour into two 8-in. round waxed paper-lined baking pans. Bake at 350° for 30-35 minutes. Cool completely. For filling, prepare pudding with milk and coffee; chill. Fold in cream. Split each cake layer and spread with filling. **Yield:** 12 servings.

EGGLESS-MILKLESS-BUTTERLESS CAKE
Jackie Noble, Pasco, Washington

This recipe came from my Grandma Frostads, who raised 12 children on a farm during the lean Depression days. It's handy during calving season when my husband and I and our three children live in a trailer with limited space for supplies.

        1 cup packed brown sugar
        1 cup water
        1 cup raisins
    1/3 cup shortening
        1 teaspoon ground cinnamon
    1/2 teaspoon ground cloves
    1/4 teaspoon ground nutmeg
        1 teaspoon baking soda
        2 tablespoons hot water
        2 cups all-purpose flour
        1 teaspoon baking powder
    1/2 teaspoon salt

In a heavy saucepan, combine first seven ingredients. Bring to a boil and boil for 5 minutes. Cool. Place in a mixing bowl. Dissolve baking soda in hot water; add to mixing bowl. Combine flour, baking powder and salt; add to batter. Pour into a greased 9-in. x 5-in. x 3-in. loaf pan. Bake at 350° for about 45 minutes or until cake tests done. Serve with **Hard Sauce** (see page 11) if desired. **Yield:** 8-10 servings.

STRAWBERRY CHIFFON CAKE
Betsy Hardt, Hope, New Jersey

This light and luscious cake, along with fresh strawberries, is a "berry good" dessert to serve at a church ice cream social.

    1 cup all-purpose flour
    3/4 cup sugar
1-1/2 teaspoons baking powder
    1/2 teaspoon salt
    1/4 cup vegetable oil
    3 eggs, *separated*
    1/3 cup orange juice
    1/4 teaspoon cream of tartar
1-1/2 to 2 quarts fresh strawberries, sliced
Vanilla ice cream
Whipped cream

Sift together flour, sugar, baking powder and salt. Place in a large bowl and make a well in the center. Add oil, egg yolks and orange juice; beat with a spoon until smooth. In a mixing bowl, beat egg whites and cream of tartar until stiff. Gradually add batter, folding gently until blended. Pour into an ungreased 9-in. x 5-in. x 3-in. loaf pan. Bake at 325° for 50-55 minutes. Invert immediately on wire rack, but keep in pan. When cool, remove cake from pan and slice into 12 pieces. Top each slice with berries, ice cream and whipped cream. **Yield:** 12 servings.

YULE LOG
Rosie Flanagan, Buchanan, Michigan
(PICTURED ON PAGE 18)

It's become a tradition to prepare this Yule Log for holiday gatherings. The filling recipe came from an aunt and the butter cream frosting was my creation. I've taught cake decorating in 4-H for 14 years, but I've been cooking since I was old enough to stand on a chair and help my mother. Now my 9-year-old granddaughter is showing interest, too!

    5 eggs, room temperature, *separated*
    2/3 cup sugar
    2 tablespoons all-purpose flour
    3 tablespoons unsweetened cocoa
FILLING:
2-1/2 tablespoons all-purpose flour
    1/2 cup milk
    1/2 cup sugar
    1/2 cup butter, softened
    1/2 teaspoon vanilla extract
    1/2 cup chopped walnuts, optional
MOCHA BUTTER CREAM FROSTING:
    1 cup butter, softened
    1/2 cup confectioners' sugar
    1 tablespoon unsweetened cocoa
    1 teaspoon strong coffee

SEASON'S EATING. Opposite page, from top to bottom: Holiday Pound Cake (p. 7), Yule Log (above), Vanilla Wafer Fruitcake (p. 21).

Confectioners' sugar, optional
Chopped nuts, optional

In a large mixing bowl, beat egg yolks at high speed until light and fluffy. Gradually add sugar, beating until mixture is thick and light-colored. Add flour and cocoa, beating on low speed. In another bowl, beat egg whites until soft peaks form; fold into batter. Mix until no streaks of white remain. Grease a 15-in. x 10-in. x 1-in. pan; line with waxed paper, and grease and flour paper. Spread batter evenly in pan. Bake at 350° for 15 minutes or until cake springs back when touched lightly. Cover with waxed paper and cool completely on wire rack. Remove paper; invert cake onto an 18-in.-long piece of waxed paper dusted with confectioners' sugar. Trim edges from all four sides of cake. For filling, combine flour and milk in a saucepan. Cook over low heat; stirring until thick. Cool. In a mixing bowl, cream sugar, butter and vanilla. Add flour mixture; beat until fluffy. Fold in walnuts if desired. Spread on cake; roll up, jelly-roll style, starting from one short end. For frosting, beat butter until fluffy in a small bowl. Beat in sugar, cocoa and coffee. Spread over cake, using a fork to create a bark-like effect. Sprinkle with confectioners' sugar and nuts if desired. **Yield:** 14-18 servings.

RED VELVET CAKE
Peg Jones, Lebanon, Indiana

We have five birthdays in our family in September, and they all request this cake! The recipe comes from my husband's Aunt Edith and makes a cake that's pretty and delicious.

    1/2 cup shortening
1-1/2 cups sugar
    2 eggs
    1/4 cup (2 ounces) red food coloring
    3 tablespoons unsweetened cocoa
2-1/4 cups all-purpose flour
    1 teaspoon baking soda
    1/2 teaspoon salt
    1 cup buttermilk
    1 tablespoon vanilla extract
    1 tablespoon vinegar
FLUFFY WHITE FROSTING:
    1 cup milk
    5 tablespoons all-purpose flour
    3/4 cup butter
    4 tablespoons shortening
1-1/2 cups sugar
    2 teaspoons vanilla extract

In a large mixing bowl, cream shortening and sugar until fluffy. Add eggs, one at a time, beating well after each addition. Combine food coloring and cocoa; add to creamed mixture. Combine flour, baking soda and salt; add alternately with buttermilk to creamed mixture. Stir in vanilla and vinegar. Pour into two 9-in. round waxed paper-lined cake pans. Bake at 350° for 35 minutes or until toothpick inserted near center comes out clean. For frosting, whisk together milk and flour in a saucepan. Cook, stirring constantly, until thick (like paste), about 5 minutes. Cool. Place in a mixing bowl with remaining ingredients. Beat at high speed until consistency of whipped cream. Frost one cake layer; top with second layer and frost entire cake. **Yield:** 12 servings.

OLD-FASHIONED STRAWBERRY SHORTCAKE
Ruth Erdmann, Monticello, Indiana
(PICTURED ON OUR COVER)

I grew up on a dairy farm, so we always had plenty of butter and cream for the luscious strawberry shortcake my mother fixed.

      1 quart fresh strawberries, sliced
      1 cup sugar
      2 cups all-purpose flour
      2 tablespoons sugar
      3 teaspoons baking powder
  1/2 teaspoon salt
  1/2 cup butter
      1 egg
  1/2 cup cream
Butter
Whipped cream

Combine strawberries and sugar; set aside. In a large bowl, sift together dry ingredients. Cut in butter until crumbly. In another bowl, beat egg; add cream. Add to crumb mixture, stirring only until moist. Pat into a greased 8-in. square or round baking pan. Bake at 450° for 15-20 minutes or until golden. Remove from pan; cool on wire rack. Just before serving, split cake in two. Butter bottom layer; spoon half of the berries over butter. Replace second layer and spoon remaining berries on top. Cut into individual servings; top each with whipped cream. **Yield:** 6-9 servings.

CARROT CAKE
Anna Aughenbaugh, Fort Collins, Colorado

We made this for our daughter's wedding. We stirred it all by hand and baked it in frying pans of varied sizes. After decorating it with pink frosting roses, we transported it 50 miles to the church in the back of a car!

1-1/3 cups vegetable oil
      4 eggs
1-1/2 cups sugar
      2 cups all-purpose flour
      2 teaspoons baking powder
      2 teaspoons baking soda
      2 teaspoons ground cinnamon
2-1/2 cups finely shredded carrots
  1/2 cup chopped walnuts
CREAM CHEESE ICING:
      1 package (3 ounces) cream cheese, softened
      3 cups confectioners' sugar
Dash salt
      1 teaspoon vanilla extract
      2 tablespoons milk

In a large mixing bowl, combine oil, eggs and sugar. Combine flour, baking powder, soda and cinnamon; add to mixing bowl. Beat well. Stir in carrots and nuts. Pour into a greased 13-in. x 9-in. x 2-in. baking pan. Bake at 350° for about 50 minutes or until cake tests done. For frosting, beat cream cheese and sugar in a medium mixing bowl. Gradually add salt, vanilla and milk, beating until smooth and spreadable. Add more milk if needed to thin frosting. Spread on cooled cake. **Yield:** 12 servings.

GRANDMA ZAUNER'S DOBOSH TORTE
Kathy Wells, Brodhead, Wisconsin

This rich torte has been a tradition in our family for many years. My mother still serves it on Christmas Eve as a birthday cake for the Christ child.

      6 eggs, *separated*
      1 cup sugar
      2 tablespoons water
      1 teaspoon vanilla extract
      1 cup all-purpose flour
      1 teaspoon baking powder
FROSTING:
  1/2 pound unsalted butter, softened
      4 squares (1 ounce *each*) semisweet chocolate, melted
      2 cups confectioners' sugar
      3 tablespoons milk
      1 teaspoon vanilla extract
      1 cup whipping cream

In a large mixing bowl, beat egg yolks and sugar very well. Add water and vanilla. Sift together flour and baking powder; add to mixing bowl. Beat egg whites until stiff; fold into batter. Pour into three 8-in. greased and floured baking pans. Bake at 350° for 15-20 minutes or until cake springs back when lightly touched. Cool and remove from pans. For frosting, beat all ingredients except cream. Stiffly whip cream and fold into frosting. Split each cake in two. Spread frosting between all layers and around entire torte. Store in refrigerator. **Yield:** 16 servings.

SOUR CREAM POUND CAKE
Karen Conrad, East Troy, Wisconsin
(PICTURED ON OUR COVER)

Because I'm our town's postmaster, I can bake only in my spare time. When I do, I especially like making desserts like this one. It tastes great as is, or tucked under ice cream and chocolate syrup like a hot fudge sundae!

      1 cup butter, softened
      3 cups sugar
      6 eggs
  1/4 teaspoon baking soda
      2 teaspoons vanilla extract
      1 cup (8 ounces) sour cream
      3 cups all-purpose flour
Confectioners' sugar, optional

In a mixing bowl, cream butter and sugar. Add eggs, one at a time, beating well after each addition. Mix baking soda and vanilla with sour cream; add alternately with flour to the creamed mixture. Mix well. Pour into a greased and floured 10-in. tube pan. Bake at 325° for 1 hour and 20 minutes or until cake tests done. Cool in pan 15 minutes before removing to a wire rack. If desired, dust with confectioners' sugar before serving. **Yield:** 16-20 servings.

STRAWBERRY SCHAUM TORTE
Geraldine Sauke, Alberta Lea, Minnesota

I've served this impressive dessert at baptisms and holidays and enjoy making it for our children and grandchildren when they come to visit.

        6 egg whites
        1 teaspoon baking powder
    1/4 teaspoon salt
        2 teaspoons vinegar
        2 teaspoons water
        2 teaspoons vanilla extract
        2 cups sugar
FILLING:
        1 package (3 ounces) strawberry-flavored
            gelatin
    1/2 cup boiling water
        1 cup fresh *or* frozen sliced strawberries
        1 teaspoon lemon juice
Dash salt
1-1/2 cups whipped cream

Place first six ingredients in a large mixing bowl. Beat at high speed. Gradually add sugar; continue beating on high until stiff peaks form. Spread evenly in a greased 13-in. x 9-in. x 2-in. baking pan. Bake at 300° for 45 minutes. Turn off oven and do not open door. Let cool in oven overnight. For filling, dissolve gelatin in water in a bowl. Stir in strawberries, lemon juice and salt (mixture will thicken quickly). Fold in cream. Spread filling over crust. Refrigerate until serving time. **Yield:** 12 servings.

GRANDMA'S APPLESAUCE CAKE
Joanie Jager, Lynden, Washington

This moist cake recipe is a treasured heirloom passed down from my Grandma Stuit, who cooked for a family of 13 during the Depression. At reunions, it's the first dessert gone...including the crumbs!

    3/4 cup raisins
        1 cup hot water
    1/2 cup shortening
        2 cups sugar
        1 egg
1-1/2 cups applesauce
2-1/2 cups all-purpose flour
    1/2 cup chopped walnuts
    1/2 teaspoon salt
    1/2 teaspoon ground cinnamon
    1/2 teaspoon ground cloves
    1/2 teaspoon ground nutmeg
        2 teaspoons baking soda
    1/2 cup boiling water
Confectioners' sugar, optional

Place raisins and hot water in a small bowl; set aside. In a large mixing bowl, combine remaining ingredients except last three. Dissolve baking soda in boiling water; add to batter. Mix well. Drain softened raisins and fold into batter. Pour into a greased and floured 13-in. x 9-in. x 2-in. baking pan. Bake at 300° for 40 minutes. If desired, dust top with confectioners' sugar. Serve warm or cold. Store in an airtight container. **Yield:** 12-16 servings.

VANILLA WAFER FRUITCAKE
Rita Bingham, Edmond, Oklahoma
(PICTURED ON PAGE 18)

This was my dear grandmother's recipe. She was a farmer's wife and a very good cook. Even folks who don't like fruitcake seem to like this one.

    1/2 pound candied cherries
    1/2 pound candied pineapple slices
        1 pound walnuts, pecans *or* combination of both
        1 pound vanilla wafers
    1/4 pound raisins
        2 eggs
    1/2 cup sugar
    1/4 teaspoon salt
        1 can (5 ounces) evaporated milk

Reserve four whole cherries, two pineapple slices and 16 pecan or walnut halves. Chop remaining fruit and nuts. Crush vanilla wafers; combine with chopped fruit, nuts and raisins and set aside. In a bowl, beat eggs well. Stir in sugar, salt and milk. Combine wafer/nut mixture with egg mixture. Pack into a waxed paper-lined angel food cake pan. Decorate top with reserved whole candy and nuts. Bake at 325° for 45 minutes. Let stand 10 minutes. Run a sharp knife around edge; turn cake out of pan, then back over again so decorations are on top. Cake can be made ahead and frozen; taste improves with age. **Yield:** about 40 servings.

LEMON BLUEBERRY TEA CAKE
Gertrude Wood, Little Valley, New York

I found this recipe in an old loose-leaf cookbook owned by my great-aunt. I've enjoyed making it for teas and afternoon get-togethers.

        1 cup fresh *or* frozen blueberries
1-2/3 cups plus 1 tablespoon all-purpose flour,
        divided
    1/2 cup butter *or* margarine, softened
        1 cup sugar
        2 eggs
1-1/2 teaspoons baking powder
    1/4 teaspoon salt
    1/2 cup milk
        1 tablespoon grated lemon peel
GLAZE:
    1/2 cup sugar
    1/4 cup lemon juice

Toss blueberries with 1 tablespoon flour; set aside. In a large mixing bowl, cream butter and sugar until light and fluffy. Add eggs, one at a time, beating well after each. Combine remaining flour with baking powder and salt; add alternately with milk to creamed mixture. Fold in lemon peel and berries. Pour into a greased and floured 9-in. x 5-in. x 3-in. loaf pan. Bake at 350° for 60-65 minutes. Meanwhile, combine glaze ingredients in a small saucepan. Heat to boiling, stirring until sugar dissolves. Cool cake in pan 10 minutes before removing to wire rack. Brush glaze on top and sides of cake. Cool. To serve, cut into 1/2-in. slices. **Yield:** 18 servings.

Cheesecakes

"When it's time for dessert, I choose cheesecake!"

WHEN company's coming, what better way to impress a guest than to serve a slice of rich, creamy cheesecake made Grandma's way?

Old-time grandmothers combined farm-fresh ingredients like milk, eggs, and ricotta, cream or cottage cheese to create this smooth, splendid dessert for visitors or relatives. Grandma would bake it in a graham-cracker or pastry crust, and for a fancy finish, she'd top it with sour cream or perhaps ripe berries brushed with melted jelly.

Cheesecake has been popular in America since the country was founded. Although George Washington is legendary for chopping down a cherry tree, it's cheesecake that he liked best—so much, in fact, that Mrs. Washington included a number of recipes for the dessert in her own cookbook! (Do you think one of the recipes called for cherry topping?)

In this chapter, you can choose from a variety of velvety cheesecakes, including delicious no-bake versions. But whether they're baked or simply chilled, these flavorful old favorites are sure to find favor with your family and friends.

CHOCOLATE GLAZED CHEESECAKE
Caryn Wiggins, Columbus, Indiana
(PICTURED ON PAGE 22)

This rich, triple-layer cheesecake is guaranteed to appeal to all dessert lovers. I've been making it for years and still receive requests for it!

    1 package (9 ounces) chocolate wafer cookies,
       crushed (about 2 cups)
 3/4 cup sugar, *divided*
 1/2 cup butter, melted
    2 packages (8 ounces *each*) and 1 package
       (3 ounces) cream cheese, softened, *divided*
    3 eggs, *divided*
    1 teaspoon vanilla extract, *divided*
    2 squares (1 ounce *each*) semisweet chocolate,
       melted and slightly cooled
1-1/3 cups sour cream, *divided*
 1/3 cup packed dark brown sugar
    1 tablespoon all-purpose flour

PRETTY AS A PICTURE. On opposite page: Chocolate Glazed Cheesecake (recipe above).

 1/4 cup chopped pecans
 1/4 teaspoon almond extract
CHOCOLATE GLAZE:
    3 squares (1 ounce *each*) semisweet chocolate
    2 tablespoons butter
 1/3 cup sifted confectioners' sugar
    1 tablespoon water
 1/2 teaspoon vanilla extract

Combine cookie crumbs, 1/4 cup sugar and butter; blend well. Press into bottom and 2 in. up the sides of a 9-in. springform pan; set aside. In a mixing bowl, beat 1 8-oz. package cream cheese and 1/4 cup sugar until fluffy. Add 1 egg and 1/4 teaspoon vanilla; blend well. Stir in chocolate and 1/3 cup sour cream. Spoon over crust. In another bowl, beat second 8-oz. package of cream cheese, brown sugar and flour until fluffy. Add 1 egg and 1/2 teaspoon vanilla; blend well. Stir in pecans. Spoon carefully over chocolate layer. In another bowl, beat remaining 3 ozs. of cream cheese and remaining sugar until fluffy. Blend in last egg. Stir in remaining sour cream and vanilla. Add almond extract. Spoon carefully over pecan layer. Bake at 325° for about 55 minutes or until center is almost set. Turn off oven and leave cheesecake inside for 30 minutes; open door partway and leave cake in oven another 30 minutes. Remove from oven; cool completely. Refrigerate at least 8 hours. For glaze, combine chocolate and butter in top of a double boiler; cook over simmering water until melted. Remove from heat; add remaining ingredients and stir until smooth. Remove cheesecake from pan and spread warm glaze on top just before serving. **Yield:** 12 servings.

GERMAN CHEESECAKE
Richard McCarthy, Linden, New Jersey

Here's an old-fashioned recipe that includes cottage cheese.

 1/2 cup graham cracker crumbs
    2 cups (16 ounces) cottage cheese
    2 packages (8 ounces *each*) cream cheese,
       softened
    1 cup sugar
    4 eggs
    1 tablespoon lemon juice
    1 teaspoon vanilla extract
 1/4 cup all-purpose flour
    2 cups (16 ounces) sour cream

Sprinkle the crumbs over the bottom and up the sides of a greased 10-in. springform pan. In a blender or food processor, puree cottage cheese; set aside. In a mixing bowl, beat cream cheese and sugar. Add eggs, one at a time, beating well after each addition. Beat in lemon juice, vanilla, flour, sour cream and pureed cottage cheese. Pour into pan. Bake at 325° for 50-60 minutes. Turn off heat and let cheesecake stand in oven for 2 hours. Do not open door. Cool. Refrigerate overnight. Slice with a wet knife. **Yield:** 16 servings.

CINNAMON CHERRY CHEESECAKE SQUARES

Vera Kramer, Jenera, Ohio
(PICTURED ON PAGE 25)

This recipe was given to me by a friend at my wedding shower 24 years ago. It has become a real family favorite over the years.

CRUST:
    24 cinnamon graham crackers, crushed
        (about 1-3/4 cups)
    1/2 cup butter *or* margarine, melted
    1/4 cup sugar
FILLING:
    2 packages (8 ounces *each*) cream cheese,
        softened
    1/2 cup sugar
    3 eggs
    1 teaspoon vanilla extract
TOPPING:
    2 cups (16 ounces) sour cream
    1/4 cup sugar
    1 teaspoon vanilla extract
    1 can (16 ounces) cherry pie filling

Combine all crust ingredients and press into the bottom of a 12-in. x 7-1/2-in. x 2-in. baking pan. For filling, beat cream cheese and sugar in a mixing bowl. Add eggs, one at a time, beating well after each addition. Add vanilla. Pour into crust; bake at 350° for 25 minutes. Meanwhile, for topping, combine the sour cream, sugar and vanilla. Spread over pie and bake an additional 5 minutes. Cool to room temperature; chill at least 4 hours. Cut into squares and top each serving with a spoonful of cherry filling. **Yield:** 12-15 servings.

FAMILY CHEESECAKE SQUARES

Loretta Ruda, Kennesaw, Georgia
(PICTURED ON PAGE 25)

Though these squares may sound time-consuming to make, they're actually quick to fix. I like serving them at room temperature, but they're good cold, too—and delicious topped with strawberries or cherry pie filling.

CRUST:
    1 package (1/4 ounce) active dry yeast
    1/4 cup warm milk (105°-110°)
    1 tablespoon sugar
2-1/2 cups all-purpose flour
    1/2 teaspoon salt
    1 cup butter *or* margarine
    4 egg yolks, lightly beaten
FILLING:
    1 egg, *separated*
    2 packages (8 ounces *each*) cream cheese
        softened
    1 cup sugar
    1 teaspoon vanilla extract
    1/2 cup chopped pecans

Dissolve yeast in warm milk; add sugar and set aside. Place

flour and salt in a large mixing bowl; cut in butter as for pie crust. Add egg yolks and yeast mixture; mix thoroughly. Divide dough into two sections. Roll each piece to fit a 13-in. x 9-in. x 2-in. baking pan. Place one piece in pan. For filling, beat egg yolk, cream cheese, sugar and vanilla until smooth. Spread over dough in pan and cover with remaining dough. Press lightly to seal edges. Lightly beat egg white; brush over top dough. Sprinkle with nuts. Cover and allow to rise in a warm place for 1-1/2 hours. Bake at 350° for 30-35 minutes or until lightly browned. **Yield:** 24 squares.

STRAWBERRY CHEESECAKE

L.C. Herschap, Luling, Texas

The creamy texture and lovely look of this cheesecake always gets compliments.

CRUST:
    3/4 cup ground pecans
    3/4 cup graham cracker crumbs
    3 tablespoons butter, melted
FILLING:
    4 packages (8 ounces *each*) cream cheese,
        softened
    4 eggs
1-1/4 cups sugar
    1 tablespoon lemon juice
    2 teaspoons vanilla extract
TOPPING:
    2 cups (16 ounces) sour cream
    1/4 cup sugar
    1 teaspoon vanilla extract
STRAWBERRY GLAZE:
    1/4 cup water
    2 tablespoons cornstarch
    1 jar (12 ounces) strawberry jelly
    3 tablespoons orange-flavored liqueur *or*
        lemon juice
Few drops red food coloring, optional
    1 quart fresh whole strawberries, hulled

Combine crust ingredients. Press into the bottom of a 10-in. springform pan; set aside. For filling, beat cream cheese in a large mixing bowl until smooth. Add eggs, sugar, lemon juice and vanilla; mix thoroughly. Spoon into crust. Bake at 350° for about 50 minutes or until filling is almost set. Remove from the oven and let stand 15 minutes. Combine topping ingredients and spread over cheesecake; return to the oven for 5 minutes. Cool to room temperature. Refrigerate 24 hours. For glaze, combine water and cornstarch in a saucepan. Add jelly and cook over medium-high heat, stirring constantly, until jelly melts and mixture thickens. Remove from heat; stir in liqueur, and food coloring if desired. Cool to room temperature. Just before serving, loosen and remove sides of pan. Arrange strawberries on top of cake with pointed ends up. Spoon glaze over berries, allowing some to drip down sides of cake. **Yield:** 12 servings.

PICNIC PICKS. On the opposite page, top to bottom: Family Cheesecake Squares (at left), Easy Mandarin Orange Cheesecake (p. 26), Cinnamon Cherry Cheesecake Squares (above).

EASY MANDARIN ORANGE CHEESECAKE
Loreen Mezei, Medicine Hat, Alberta
(PICTURED ON PAGE 25)

Since I'm a working mom with three young children and a husband who farms, time in the kitchen is precious. This dessert is not only easy to make, it's also pretty to look at and delicious to eat!

CRUST:
>   1 cup graham cracker crumbs
>   (about 14 crackers)
>   1/4 cup sugar
>   1/4 cup butter *or* margarine, melted

FILLING:
>   2 packages (8 ounces *each*) cream cheese,
>   softened
>   1 cup sugar
>   1/4 cup frozen orange juice concentrate, thawed
>   2 teaspoons orange extract
>   1 cup whipping cream, whipped
>   2 teaspoons grated orange peel, optional
>   1 can (11 ounces) mandarin orange sections,
>   drained and patted dry

Combine crust ingredients and press into the bottom of a 9-in. pie plate. Bake at 350° for 6-8 minutes or until lightly browned. Cool. Meanwhile, for filling, beat cream cheese and sugar in a mixing bowl until light and fluffy. Add concentrate and extract; beat well. Fold in whipped cream, and orange peel if desired. Spread evenly into crust. Arrange oranges in decorative design on top of filling. Chill at least 3 hours. **Yield:** 8 servings.

APPLE CHEESECAKE
Barbara Martin Thompson, Pollock Pines, California

This apple dessert represents my area of the country—and it's definitely delicious!

CRUST:
1-1/2 cups graham cracker crumbs
>   1/2 cup sugar
>   1/3 cup butter *or* margarine, melted

APPLE TOPPING:
>   1/2 cup sugar
>   1/2 cup lemon juice
>   1 tablespoon all-purpose flour
>   1/2 teaspoon ground cinnamon

Dash ground nutmeg
>   6 Granny Smith *or* other baking apples, peeled,
>   cored and thinly sliced
>   1/2 cup chopped pecans

FILLING:
>   3 packages (8 ounces *each*) cream cheese,
>   softened
>   3 eggs
>   3/4 cup sugar
1-1/2 teaspoons vanilla extract

Combine crust ingredients; press into the bottom and 1-1/2 in. up the sides of a 9-in. springform pan. Refrigerate. For topping, place sugar, lemon juice, flour, cinnamon and nutmeg in a Dutch oven; mix well. Add apples. Bring

to a boil; cover and simmer 15 minutes or just until apples are tender, gently stirring as needed. Remove from the heat; carefully fold in pecans. Cool to room temperature. Set aside 3 tablespoons; refrigerate the rest until serving time. For filling, combine cream cheese, eggs, sugar and vanilla in a large mixing bowl; mix until well blended. Add 3 tablespoons reserved topping; mix well. Pour filling into crust. Bake at 350° for 50 minutes. Turn oven off, but leave cheesecake in oven with door ajar for 1 hour. Cool to room temperature; chill at least 4 hours. Before serving, top with apple topping. **Yield:** 12 servings.

RASPBERRY SUPREME CHEESECAKE
Linda Ward, Newton, Iowa

When I take this fruity, flavorful cheesecake to work, the pan is licked clean in no time at all! I never had a recipe for it, so when co-workers asked for it, I had to write down the recipe as I made it the next time.

>   2 cups graham cracker crumbs
>   1 cup chopped toasted almonds
>   1/2 cup sugar
>   2/3 cup butter, melted
>   1 package (8 ounces) cream cheese, softened
>   1 can (14 ounces) sweetened condensed milk
>   1/3 cup lemon juice
>   1 teaspoon vanilla extract
>   1 package (6 ounces) raspberry-flavored
>   gelatin
>   2 cups hot water
>   2 packages (10 ounces *each*) frozen
>   raspberries, partially thawed
>   2 cups whipped cream
>   1/4 cup toasted slivered almonds

Combine first four ingredients. Press into the bottom of a 13-in. x 9-in. x 2-in. baking pan; chill for 30 minutes. Meanwhile, beat cream cheese, milk, lemon juice and vanilla until smooth. Pour over crust; chill. Dissolve gelatin in water. Add raspberries and stir until completely thawed; chill until very thick. Pour over filling. Chill until set. Before serving, top with whipped cream and almonds. Store in refrigerator. **Yield:** 16-20 servings.

TROPICAL CHEESECAKE
Delores Mason, Jacksonville, Illinois

This recipe has been a favorite of mine for years because of its easy preparation. It makes a sweet and light dessert.

>   1 package (8 ounces) cream cheese, softened
>   1/2 cup confectioners' sugar
>   1 can (8 ounces) crushed pineapple, drained
>   1 package (3 ounces) dessert topping mix
>   1/2 cup cold milk
>   1/2 teaspoon vanilla extract
>   1 graham cracker crust (8 inches)

In a mixing bowl, beat cream cheese and sugar until fluffy. Stir in pineapple. In another bowl, combine dessert topping mix with milk and vanilla; beat until stiff. Fold into pineapple mixture. Spread evenly in crust. Chill. **Yield:** 8-10 servings.

FROM GRANDMA'S KITCHEN:
Chocolate Swirl Cheesecake

Aida D. Babbel

*"My grandma made this recipe,
my mom made it and now I make it!"*

Whenever Aida Babbel of Coquitlam, British Columbia serves Chocolate Swirl Cheesecake to her family or guests, it disappears quickly. But the warm memories of making this luscious dessert with her grandmother linger on long after the plates are empty.

"I have all these wonderful memories—even as a teenager—of being around my grandmother. She would say, 'Here, you've got to learn how to cook and houseclean to make your future husband happy,'" Aida recalls.

Aida and her mother would drive 45 minutes, then take a 2-hour ferry ride to Vancouver Island to visit Grandma, who originally immigrated to Canada from Ukraine.

" 'Baba' (that's Ukrainian for Grandma) and my mother were very close, so we went to Baba's house and cooked together a lot," says Aida, who is the youngest of nine children.

The cheesecake recipe was one of many passed down by Baba, but it didn't originate in Ukraine.

In the early 1900's, Aida's grandparents owned a logging company, and Baba cooked daily for the large camp of German immigrant workers. In broken English, she asked them about their favorite foods and managed to gather recipes for sauerbraten, headcheese and other German dishes, including Chocolate Swirl

Cheesecake. The first time she made the cheesecake, though, she misinterpreted the instructions and put in 2 *dozen* eggs!

Through trial and error, the recipe was fine-tuned, first by Baba, and later by Aida's mother, who wanted to impress her husband's boss to ensure a raise. "My mother went over to her neighbor's house. Together they worked on the recipe and decided to add orange juice," Aida recalls. "After my mother served the cheesecake, Dad got that raise!"

Aida has made about 30 different cheesecake recipes but prefers Chocolate Swirl Cheesecake for its taste and ease of preparation. She loves baking and has carried on the tradition of serving it to her dessert-loving family for Christmas and other special occasions. "Rarely does anyone have only one piece of this," Aida reports. "My husband always has three at a sitting, and our three daughters would, too— only I don't let them!"

CHOCOLATE SWIRL CHEESECAKE

1/3 cup graham cracker crumbs
4 packages (8 ounces *each*) cream cheese, softened
1-1/3 cups sugar
4 eggs
2 tablespoons orange juice
2 teaspoons grated orange peel
3 squares (1 ounce *each*) semisweet chocolate, melted
Whipped cream, optional

Sprinkle crumbs over bottom and sides of a lightly greased 9-in. springform pan. In a large mixing bowl, beat cream cheese until light and fluffy. Add sugar; beat 1 minute. Add eggs, one at a time, beating well after each addition. Add orange juice and peel; beat at medium speed for 2-3 minutes. Reserve 1-1/4 cups filling and pour remaining into pan. Blend chocolate into reserved filling, then drop by spoonfuls over filling in pan and swirl with a knife. Place on middle oven rack with a pan of water on lower rack. Bake at 350° for 55-60 minutes or until set. Turn oven off and allow cheesecake to sit for 2 hours. Refrigerate 3-4 hours or overnight. Carefully remove sides of pan before cutting. Serve with whipped cream if desired. **Yield:** 12-16 servings.

PUMPKIN CHEESECAKE

Evonne Wurmnest, Normal, Illinois

(PICTURED ON PAGE 28)

When I was young, we produced several ingredients for this longtime favorite on the farm. We raised pumpkins in our large vegetable garden, and made homemade butter and lots of sour cream from our dairy herd.

CRUST:
    1 cup graham cracker crumbs
    1 tablespoon sugar
    4 tablespoons butter *or* margarine, melted
FILLING:
    2 packages (8 ounces *each*) cream cheese, softened
    3/4 cup sugar
    1 can (16 ounces) pumpkin
1-1/4 teaspoons ground cinnamon
    1/2 teaspoon ground ginger
    1/2 teaspoon ground nutmeg
    1/4 teaspoon salt
    2 eggs
TOPPING:
    2 cups (16 ounces) sour cream
    2 tablespoons sugar
    1 teaspoon vanilla extract
    12 to 16 pecan halves

Combine crust ingredients. Press into bottom of a 9-in. springform pan; chill. For filling, beat cream cheese and sugar in a large mixing bowl until well blended. Beat in pumpkin, spices and salt. Add eggs, one at a time, beating well after each. Pour into crust. Bake at 350° for 50 minutes. Meanwhile, for topping, combine sour cream, sugar and vanilla. Spread over filling; bake 5 minutes more. Cool on rack; chill overnight. Garnish each slice with a pecan half. **Yield:** 12-16 servings.

ROYAL RASPBERRY CHEESECAKE

Lori Manthorpe, Ile Bizard, Quebec

This recipe reminds me of a cheesecake I often enjoyed at a restaurant in British Columbia, where I used to live. It's fit for a king!

CRUST:
    3/4 cup all-purpose flour
    3 tablespoons sugar
    1/2 teaspoon finely grated lemon peel
    6 tablespoons butter
    1 egg yolk, lightly beaten
    1/4 teaspoon vanilla extract
FILLING:
    3 packages (8 ounces *each*) cream cheese, softened
    1/2 teaspoon finely grated lemon peel

HOLIDAY HARVEST. On the opposite page, Cranberry Cheesecake (p. 31), Pumpkin Cheesecake (above).

    1/4 teaspoon vanilla extract
    1 cup sugar
    2 tablespoons all-purpose flour
    1/4 teaspoon salt
    2 eggs
    1 egg yolk
    1/4 cup milk
RASPBERRY SAUCE:
    1 package (10 ounces) frozen raspberries, thawed and crushed
    1 tablespoon cornstarch
    1/2 cup black *or* red currant jelly
TOPPING:
    3 cups fresh *or* frozen whole raspberries

In a mixing bowl, combine flour, sugar and lemon peel. Cut in butter until crumbly. Stir in egg yolk and vanilla. Pat 1/3 of mixture on the bottom of a 9-in. springform pan with the sides removed. Bake at 400° for 7 minutes or until golden; cool. Attach the sides of the pan; pat remaining crust mixture 1-3/4 in. up the sides. Set aside. For filling, beat cream cheese, lemon peel and vanilla until fluffy. Combine sugar, flour and salt; add to creamed mixture, beating well. Add eggs and yolk; beat at a low speed just until combined. Stir in milk. Pour into crust. Place on a shallow baking pan in oven. Bake at 375° for 35-40 minutes or until center appears set. Cool for 15 minutes. Loosen sides of cheesecake from pan with a spatula; cool 30 minutes. Remove sides of pan; cool 1-2 hours longer. Chill thoroughly. Meanwhile, for sauce, combine all ingredients in a saucepan. Cook and stir over medium heat until thickened and bubbly. Cook and stir 1 minute more. Remove from heat; strain to remove berry seeds. Cool. Just before serving, top cheesecake with sauce and whole berries. **Yield:** 12 servings.

FROZEN MOCHA CHEESECAKE

Sharon Marskamp, St. George, Ontario

This dessert is oh-so-rich and handy to have in the freezer for unexpected company (like we had last night!). I grew up with eight brothers who devoured a cake every day! That meant my mother and I spent many evenings in the kitchen...and we never heard of cake mixes back then!

CRUST:
1-1/2 cups chocolate wafer crumbs
    2 tablespoons sugar
    1/3 cup butter *or* margarine, melted
FILLING:
    2 packages (8 ounces *each*) cream cheese, softened
    1 can (14 ounces) sweetened condensed milk
    2/3 cup chocolate syrup
    1 tablespoon instant coffee granules
    1 teaspoon hot water
    1 cup whipped cream

Combine crust ingredients. Press into the bottom of a 9-in. springform pan; set aside. For filling, beat cream cheese in a large mixing bowl until smooth. Gradually add milk and syrup. Dissolve coffee in water; add to mixing bowl. Fold in whipped cream. Pour into crust; freeze at least 6 hours. **Yield:** 12-16 servings.

PEANUT BUTTER CHEESE TORTE
Ruth Blair, Waukesha, Wisconsin

This dessert has long been a favorite of my family's. I especially like the fact that it requires no baking—and who doesn't like peanut butter with chocolate?

CRUST:
- 1 cup graham cracker crumbs
- 1/4 cup packed brown sugar
- 1/4 cup butter *or* margarine, melted
- 1/2 cup finely chopped peanuts

FILLING:
- 2 cups creamy peanut butter
- 2 packages (8 ounces *each*) cream cheese, softened
- 2 cups sugar
- 2 tablespoons butter *or* margarine, softened
- 2 teaspoons vanilla extract
- 1-1/2 cups whipping cream, stiffly beaten

CHOCOLATE TOPPING:
- 4 ounces semisweet chocolate chips
- 3 tablespoons plus 2 teaspoons hot coffee

Coarsely chopped peanuts, optional

Combine all crust ingredients. Press into the bottom and halfway up the sides of a 10-in. springform pan. Chill. For filling, beat peanut butter, cream cheese, sugar, butter and vanilla in a large mixing bowl on high until smooth, about 2 minutes. Fold in whipped cream. Gently spoon into crust; refrigerate 6 hours or overnight. For topping, melt chocolate with coffee until smooth. Spread over chilled torte. Refrigerate until firm, about 30 minutes. Garnish with peanuts if desired. **Yield:** 14-16 servings.

SIMPLIFIED WEIGHTS AND MEASURES	
3 teaspoons	1 tablespoon
4 tablespoons	1/4 cup
5-1/3 tablespoons	1/3 cup
8 tablespoons	1/2 cup
12 tablespoons	3/4 cup
16 tablespoons	1 cup or 1/2 pint
2 cups	1 pint
4 cups	2 pints or 1 quart
4 cups flour	1 pound
2-1/4 cups granulated sugar	1 pound
2 cups packed brown sugar	1 pound
3-1/2 cups confectioners' sugar	1 pound
2 tablespoons butter	1 ounce
8 tablespoons butter	1 stick
1 stick butter	1/2 cup
1/2 cup butter	1/4 pound
2 cups butter	1 pound
8-10 egg whites	1 cup
14 egg yolks	1 cup
Juice of 1 medium lemon	3 tablespoons

CHERRY CHEESE PIE
Lennis Sigrist, Pine Island, Minnesota

I've been making this dessert for my husband and family for years. It mixes up in a jiffy!

- 1 package (8 ounces) cream cheese, softened
- 1/3 cup sugar
- 1 cup (8 ounces) sour cream
- 2 teaspoons vanilla extract
- 1 carton (8 ounces) frozen whipped topping, thawed
- 1 graham cracker crust (9 inches)

Cherry pie filling

In a mixing bowl, beat cream cheese until smooth. Gradually add sugar. Blend in sour cream and vanilla. Fold in whipped topping. Spoon into crust; chill until set, at least 4 hours. Top with pie filling; chill until ready to serve. **Yield:** 8 servings. **Variation:** Instead of topping with fruit filling, fold chocolate chips into the cheesecake after adding whipped topping.

OLD-WORLD RICOTTA CHEESECAKE
Mary Beth Jung, Grafton, Wisconsin

I reconstructed this dessert based on an old recipe that had been in the family for years but was never written down. The subtle cinnamon flavor of the zwieback crust and the dense texture of the ricotta cheese are reminiscent of the cheesecake I enjoyed as a child.

ZWIEBACK CRUST:
- 1-2/3 cups zwieback crumbs
- 1/2 teaspoon ground cinnamon
- 3 tablespoons sugar
- 1/3 cup butter *or* margarine, softened

FILLING:
- 2 cartons (15 ounces *each*) ricotta cheese
- 1/2 cup half-and-half cream
- 1/2 cup sugar
- 2 tablespoons all-purpose flour
- 1 tablespoon lemon juice
- 1 teaspoon finely grated lemon peel
- 1/4 teaspoon salt
- 2 eggs

TOPPING:
- 1 cup (8 ounces) sour cream
- 2 tablespoons sugar
- 1 teaspoon vanilla extract

Combine crust ingredients; press over the bottom and 1-1/2 in. up the sides of a 9-in. springform pan. Chill. Meanwhile, for filling, combine ricotta cheese, cream, sugar, flour, lemon juice, peel and salt in a mixing bowl. Blend until smooth. Add eggs, one at a time, beating well after each addition. Pour into crust. Bake at 350° for 50 minutes or until center is set. For topping, beat all ingredients in a small mixing bowl. Gently spread over warm cheesecake. Return to oven for 10 minutes. Turn off oven; cool cheesecake in oven with door propped open for 30 minutes. Remove to a wire rack to cool completely. Chill for at least 3 hours. **Yield:** 12 servings.

⊱♥♥♥⊰

CRANBERRY CHEESECAKE
Nairda Monroe, Webberville, Michigan
(PICTURED ON PAGE 28)

Every year when the cranberries are harvested, my family looks forward to eating this cheesecake.

    2 cups graham cracker *or* shortbread cookie
      crumbs
    1/3 cup butter *or* margarine, melted
CRANBERRY TOPPING:
    1/3 cup water
    2/3 cup sugar
    2 cups fresh cranberries
    1 teaspoon lemon juice
FILLING:
    4 packages (8 ounces *each*) cream cheese,
      softened
    1 cup sugar
    5 eggs
    1 tablespoon lemon juice

Combine crumbs and butter; press into the bottom of a 9-in. springform pan. Bake at 300° for 5-8 minutes. Cool. Meanwhile, for topping, combine water and sugar in a saucepan. Bring to a boil over medium heat; boil 1 minute. Stir in berries; cover and reduce heat. Cook until most berries have popped, about 3 minutes. Add lemon juice. Press mixture through a sieve or food mill; set aside. For filling, beat cream cheese in a large mixing bowl until light. Gradually beat in sugar. Add eggs, one at a time, beating well after each. Add lemon juice. Pour into crust; spoon 4 tablespoons topping on filling and "marble" with a knife or spatula. Bake at 350° for 45 minutes. Turn oven off; let cake stand in oven 2 hours. Remove from oven; cool. Pour remaining topping on top; refrigerate overnight. **Yield:** 12-16 servings.

⊱♥♥♥⊰

LUSCIOUS LEMON CHEESECAKE
Shirley Connolley, Berwyn, Alberta

This creamy cheesecake is heavenly...and convenient for busy farmers like us. When we have company coming, I make it the day before.

CRUST:
2-2/3 cups graham cracker crumbs
    1/2 cup confectioners' sugar
1-1/2 teaspoons grated lemon peel
    1/2 cup butter, softened
FILLING:
    5 packages (8 ounces *each*) cream cheese,
      softened
1-3/4 cups sugar

    3 tablespoons all-purpose flour
1-1/2 teaspoons grated lemon peel
    1 teaspoon vanilla extract
    5 eggs, lightly beaten
    2 egg yolks, lightly beaten
    1/4 cup whipping cream
Fresh *or* frozen strawberries, optional

In a bowl, combine crust ingredients with a fork. Reserve 3/4 cup of mixture; sprinkle remaining crumbs evenly onto the bottom and sides of a 10-in. springform pan. For filling, beat cream cheese, sugar, flour, lemon peel and vanilla in a large mixing bowl. Gradually add eggs and yolks, beating well. Blend in whipping cream. Spread evenly into pan. Sprinkle reserved crumbs on top. Bake at 250° for 1 hour. Turn off heat and leave cheesecake in oven 1 hour longer. Remove to wire rack to cool 4-6 hours. Refrigerate overnight. Garnish with strawberries if desired. **Yield:** 16-20 servings.

> **DOUBLE TROUBLE:** If you use a double boiler to melt chocolate, be careful not to get water in the chocolate—it will harden. If you don't own a double boiler, place water in a large saucepan, then set a smaller saucepan with the chocolate inside it and heat on low.

⊱♥♥♥⊰

ICEBOX COOKIE CHEESECAKE
Perlene Hoekema, Lynden, Washington

Cookie lovers will come back for "seconds" when you serve this tempting treat.

1-1/4 cups chocolate wafer crumbs
    4 tablespoons butter *or* margarine, melted
    2 cups whipping cream, *divided*
    3 packages (8 ounces *each*) cream cheese,
      softened
    1 cup sugar
1-1/4 pounds cream-filled chocolate cookies
      (54 cookies), *divided*
    4 squares (1 ounce *each*) semisweet chocolate
    1/2 teaspoon vanilla extract
Whipped cream

Combine crumbs and butter; press into bottom of a 9-in. or 10-in. springform pan. Freeze. Whip 1-1/2 cups whipping cream until stiff peaks form; refrigerate. In a large mixing bowl, beat cream cheese until smooth. Gradually add sugar; blend thoroughly. Break 38 of the cookies each into three pieces; fold into filling along with chilled whipped cream. Spread filling evenly into crust, smoothing top and spreading to edges. Cover and refrigerate 4 hours or overnight. Meanwhile, melt chocolate in a saucepan over low heat, stirring constantly. Remove from heat; cool slightly. Whisk in vanilla and remaining whipping cream. Loosen cheesecake from pan by running knife around edge; remove from pan. Glaze top and sides of cake with chocolate mixture. Refrigerate until glaze hardens, about 30 minutes. To serve, cut into 16 pieces; top each piece with a dollop of whipped cream and stand a whole cookie upright in cream. **Yield:** 16 servings.

Cobblers, Crisps & Kuchens

"I'd walk a mile or more for one of Grandma's down-home desserts!"

LEAVE it to our grandmothers to create unforgettable desserts with names as equally unforgettable—cobbler, pandowdy, betty and slump...or how about fritter, kuchen, buckle and grunt?

The truth is, there's a reason—sometimes more than one—for each of these odd, old-fashioned names. Large dollops of biscuit dough dropped over fruit, for example, created a cobblestone effect... thus, a cobbler! And when Grandma would "cobble up" a homemade cobbler, that meant she was putting it together in a hurry. (Of course, people would *gobble* it up in a hurry, too!)

A berry "grunt" was named for the gurgling noise it made as it steamed in a big kettle hanging over an open fire. Louisa May Alcott, author of *Little Women*, called her Massachusetts' home Apple Slump, but the name actually refers to a type of stove-top apple cobbler. Its crust "slumps" down when the fruit cooks.

No matter what the name, though, you can now enjoy Grandma's steaming dumplings and fruit, deep-fried fritters, coffee cakes and fruit-filled pastries to your heart's content. You'll find the recipes in this chapter just right for scrumptious Sunday brunches, tasty after-school treats or delicious desserts when company's coming.

APPLE CRISP
June Smith, Byron Center, Michigan
(PICTURED ON PAGE 32)

Delicious with ice cream or plain for breakfast, this dessert serves a crowd. It's perfect for picnics and family gatherings.

        3 quarts sliced pared apples (about 12
          medium)
        2 cups sugar
        2 teaspoons ground cinnamon
    1/2 teaspoon ground nutmeg
    1/2 cup shortening

NATURALLY NOSTALGIC. On the opposite page, from top to bottom: Cranberry-Apple Nut Crunch (p. 34), Apple Crisp (above), Blueberry Slump (p. 34).

    1/2 cup butter *or* margarine, softened
        1 cup packed brown sugar
1-1/2 cups all-purpose flour
1-1/2 cups rolled oats
    1/2 teaspoon baking soda
    1/2 teaspoon salt
Ice cream, optional

Place apples, sugar, cinnamon and nutmeg in a saucepan; cook and stir just until apples are softened. Set aside. In a mixing bowl, cream shortening, butter and brown sugar. Combine flour, oats, baking soda and salt; add to creamed mixture. Pat half of flour mixture in the bottom of a greased 13-in. x 9-in. x 2-in. baking pan. Spread apples over top, then crumble remaining flour mixture over apples. Bake at 400° for 25-30 minutes or until golden brown. Serve warm with ice cream if desired. **Yield:** about 16 servings.

STREUSEL COFFEE CAKE
Mrs. Jim Blemker, Holland, Indiana

Here's a moist coffee cake with a nutty streusel topping.

    1/2 cup butter *or* margarine
    3/4 cup sugar
        1 teaspoon vanilla extract
        3 eggs
        2 cups all-purpose flour
        1 teaspoon baking powder
        1 teaspoon baking soda
        1 cup (8 ounces) sour cream
STREUSEL TOPPING:
        1 cup chopped pecans
        1 cup packed brown sugar
    1/2 teaspoon ground cinnamon
        6 tablespoons butter *or* margarine, softened
ICING:
        1 cup sifted confectioners' sugar
        1 tablespoon butter *or* margarine, softened
    1/2 teaspoon vanilla extract
        3 tablespoons milk

In a mixing bowl, cream butter for 30 seconds. Add sugar and vanilla; beat until well combined. Add eggs, one at a time, beating well after each addition. Combine flour, baking powder and soda; add to creamed mixture alternately with sour cream. Spoon half of batter into a greased 10-in. tube pan. Combine topping ingredients; sprinkle half over batter. Add remaining batter and topping. Bake at 350° for 45 minutes or until done. Cool in pan on wire rack for 10 minutes before removing from pan to cool completely. For icing, combine all ingredients; drizzle over cake. **Yield:** 12-14 servings.

SOUR CREAM RHUBARB COFFEE CAKE
Arlene Vogt, Fond du Lac, Wisconsin

Our daughter Judy won a blue ribbon with this recipe at the New York State Fair when we were living in Upstate New York. It's been a family favorite for 18 years.

1-1/2 cups packed brown sugar
1/2 cup shortening
1 egg
2 cups all-purpose flour
1 teaspoon baking soda
1/2 teaspoon salt
1 cup (8 ounces) sour cream
1-1/2 cups chopped rhubarb (1/2-inch chunks)
TOPPING:
1/2 cup sugar
1/2 cup chopped walnuts
1 teaspoon ground cinnamon
1 tablespoon butter, softened

In a mixing bowl, cream sugar, shortening and egg. Combine flour, baking soda and salt; add to creamed mixture alternately with sour cream. Gently fold in rhubarb until evenly distributed. Spoon into a greased 13-in. x 9-in. x 2-in. baking pan. Combine topping ingredients until crumbly; sprinkle over batter. Bake at 350° for 45-50 minutes or until done. Cool slightly before cutting into squares. **Yield:** 12-15 servings.

BLUEBERRY SLUMP
Eleanore Ebeling, Brewster, Minnesota
(PICTURED ON PAGE 32)

My mother-in-law used to make slump with wild blueberries and serve it warm with a pitcher of farm cream on the table. My husband and I have been eating it for 58 years, but the recipe is even older!

3 cups fresh *or* frozen blueberries
1/2 cup sugar
1-1/4 cups water
1 teaspoon finely grated lemon peel
1 tablespoon lemon juice
1 cup all-purpose flour
2 tablespoons sugar
2 teaspoons baking powder
1/2 teaspoon salt
1 tablespoon butter *or* margarine
1/2 cup milk
Cream *or* whipped cream, optional

In a large heavy saucepan, combine blueberries, sugar, water, lemon peel and juice; bring to a boil. Reduce heat and simmer, uncovered, for 5 minutes. Meanwhile, combine flour, sugar, baking powder and salt; cut in butter until mixture resembles a coarse meal. Add milk quickly, mixing until dry ingredients are just moistened. Drop dough by spoonfuls into simmering berries (makes six dumplings). Cover and cook over low heat for 10 minutes. Do not lift lid. Spoon dumplings into individual serving bowls and spoon some sauce over each. Serve warm with cream or whipped cream if desired. **Yield:** 6 servings.

CRANBERRY-APPLE NUT CRUNCH
Joyce Sheets, Lafayette, Indiana
(PICTURED ON PAGE 32)

This dessert is especially pretty and appropriate for the holidays. I updated my mother's recipe using instant oatmeal to make it even easier to fix.

3 cups chopped peeled apples
2 cups fresh *or* frozen cranberries
3 tablespoons all-purpose flour
1 cup sugar
TOPPING:
3 packages (1.62 ounces *each*) instant oatmeal with cinnamon and spice
3/4 cup chopped pecans
1/2 cup all-purpose flour
1/2 cup packed brown sugar
1/2 cup butter, melted
Whole cranberries for garnish
Vanilla ice cream, optional

In a large bowl, combine first four ingredients and mix well. Place in a 2-qt. baking dish; set aside. For topping, combine oatmeal, nuts, flour, sugar and butter in another bowl. Mix well; spoon evenly over fruit mixture. Bake, uncovered, at 350° for 50-60 minutes or until fruit is bubbly and tender. Garnish with cranberries. Serve warm with ice cream if desired. **Yield:** 8 servings.

CHERRY RHUBARB CRUNCH
Sharon Wasikowski, Middleville, Michigan

This recipe—along with a bundle of rhubarb—was given to me by my husband's grandmother when we were first married. I had never cared for rhubarb, but after trying this dessert, I changed my mind. Now my children dig in, too!

1 cup rolled oats
1 cup packed brown sugar
1 cup all-purpose flour
1/4 teaspoon salt
1/2 cup butter *or* margarine
4 cups diced rhubarb
1 cup sugar
2 tablespoons cornstarch
1 cup water
1 teaspoon almond extract
1 can (21 ounces) cherry pie filling
1/2 cup finely chopped walnuts

In a large mixing bowl, combine oats, brown sugar, flour and salt; stir well. Cut in butter until crumbly. Pat 2 cups of mixture into a greased 13-in. x 9-in. x 2-in. baking pan; cover with rhubarb. In a saucepan, combine sugar and cornstarch. Stir in water; cook until mixture is thickened and clear. Stir in extract and cherry filling; spoon over rhubarb. Combine nuts with reserved crumb mixture; sprinkle over cherries. Bake at 350° for about 40-45 minutes. **Yield:** 12-15 servings.

PEACH BLUEBERRY COBBLER
Ramona Banfield, Harrison, Arkansas

I once made a triple recipe of this cobbler for a picnic and it was still warm when I served it. Everyone loved it!

FILLING:
>   2 cups fresh *or* frozen sliced peaches
>   1/3 to 1/2 cup sugar
>   4 teaspoons quick-cooking tapioca
>   2 teaspoons lemon juice
>   1 cup fresh *or* frozen blueberries

Ground nutmeg
DUMPLINGS:
>   1 cup (rounded) all-purpose flour
>   2 tablespoons sugar

1-1/2 teaspoons baking powder
>   1/8 teaspoon salt
>   1 teaspoon grated lemon peel
>   1/4 cup butter *or* margarine
>   1/2 cup cream *or* evaporated milk

Vanilla ice cream, optional

In a 1-1/2-qt. baking dish, combine peaches, sugar, tapioca and lemon juice. Sprinkle blueberries over top. Sprinkle with nutmeg; set aside. For dumplings, combine first five ingredients in a mixing bowl; cut in butter with a pastry blender until mixture resembles cornmeal. Add cream or milk; stir until dough is mixed and moistened. Drop by tablespoonfuls over fruit mixture. Sprinkle nutmeg over dumplings. Bake at 400° for 25-30 minutes or until top is golden brown. Serve warm with ice cream if desired. **Yield:** 8 servings.

PEAR COFFEE CAKE
Hazyl Lindley, Abilene, Texas

I first tasted a moist, delicious pear coffee cake at a bake sale. At Christmas, I bake it instead of fruitcake, adding chopped nuts and chopped red and green candied cherries—about 1/4 cup of each.

>   2 cups sugar

1-1/2 cups vegetable oil
>   3 eggs
>   3 cups all-purpose flour
>   1 teaspoon ground cinnamon
>   1 teaspoon salt
>   1 teaspoon baking soda
>   2 teaspoons vanilla extract
>   2 cups flaked coconut
>   1 cup chopped dates
>   3 cups chopped peeled pears
>   1 cup pecans, chopped

In a mixing bowl, cream together sugar and oil. Add eggs, one at a time, beating well after each addition. Sift together flour, cinnamon, salt and baking soda; add to creamed mixture. Add vanilla. By hand, stir in coconut, dates, pears and pecans (batter will be thick). Spoon into a greased and floured fluted tube pan. Bake at 325° for 1-1/2 to 2 hours or until cake tests done. Cool on rack until cake comes away from sides of pan; remove from pan to a wire rack to cool completely. **Yield:** 16 servings.

TILLIE'S GINGER CRUMB CAKE
Kathy Nienow Clark, Byron, Michigan

This recipe goes back at least as far as my grandmother, who was born in the early 1900's. Our sons and I enjoy eating it in a bowl with milk poured on it—much to the dismay of my husband, who prefers it plain!

>   4 cups all-purpose flour
>   2 cups sugar
>   1 cup butter
>   1/2 teaspoon ground ginger
>   1/4 teaspoon ground cloves
>   1/2 teaspoon ground cinnamon
>   1/2 teaspoon ground nutmeg
>   1 cup plus 2 tablespoons buttermilk *or*
>   sour milk

1-1/4 teaspoons baking soda
>   2 eggs

Combine flour and sugar; cut in butter until crumbly. Reserve 2 cups; combine remaining crumb mixture with all remaining ingredients. Sprinkle 1 cup reserved crumbs in the bottom of a greased 13-in. x 9-in. x 2-in. baking pan. Pour batter over crumbs and sprinkle remaining crumbs on top. Bake at 350° for about 35 minutes or until a toothpick inserted near the center comes out clean. **Yield:** 16-20 servings.

It Was a Dark and Stormy Night...

The winds were howling and the snow had been falling steadily for hours. My brother and four sisters and I huddled around as Grandma stoked up the wood-burning stove...that's when she whipped up some of the best desserts I've ever tasted!

During one such storm in the early '30's, Grandma put wild blackberries (that she'd picked and canned the previous summer) into a large kettle to cook and thicken on the stove. Into that bubbling blackberry brew, she dropped large spoonfuls of soft dough.

Soon our soup plates were filled with plump purple dumplings swimming in a sea of juice and berries. Warm and cozy, we let the storm rage outside, while inside, the berries reminded us that summer would be along soon enough.

On another snowy night, Grandma asked us to bring in extra armfuls of wood, so the stove could be made hotter for baking. Then we set to peeling a bucket of apples. (The peels were made into jam for fried bread dough in the summer.)

Grandma arranged the cut-up apples in a large pan, topped them with sugar and laid a thick blanket of dough on top, sprinkling cinnamon over all. When this was baked a golden brown, we knew our favorite "Apple Betty" was ready.

Grandma filled our plates with Apple Betty and poured warmed milk (never cold) just inside the rim, so it would circle all around. Ummmm! I did so enjoy those stormy-night desserts!
—*Muriel G. Bordis, Gloversville, New York*

BLUEBERRY BUCKLE
Jo-Anne Stacey, Kelligrews, Newfoundland

I love the flavor of this old-fashioned fruity dessert.

      1/4 cup shortening
      1/2 cup sugar
        1 egg
        1 cup all-purpose flour
1-1/2 teaspoons baking powder
      1/2 teaspoon salt
      1/2 cup milk
        2 cups fresh *or* frozen blueberries
TOPPING:
      1/4 cup butter
      1/2 cup sugar
      1/3 cup all-purpose flour
      1/2 teaspoon ground cinnamon

In a medium mixing bowl, cream shortening and sugar. Beat in egg. Combine flour, baking powder and salt; add alternately with milk to creamed mixture. Pour into an ungreased 8-in. square baking pan. Arrange blueberries on top. In another mixing bowl, cream butter and sugar. Combine flour and cinnamon; add gradually to creamed mixture. Crumble over blueberries. Bake at 350° for 45-50 minutes. **Yield:** 8 servings.

> **COLD CREAM:** To prepare perfect whipped cream, chill the cream, bowl and beaters before whipping.

APPLE PANDOWDY
Doreen Lindquist, Thompson, Manitoba

This dessert, which comes from a very old cookbook, is tangy and delicious.

        1 cup packed brown sugar
1-1/4 cups all-purpose flour, *divided*
      1/2 teaspoon salt, *divided*
        1 cup water
        1 teaspoon lemon juice
        2 teaspoons baking powder
        5 tablespoons butter, *divided*
      3/4 cup milk
        5 cups sliced pared apples
      1/2 teaspoon ground cinnamon
      1/2 teaspoon ground nutmeg
        1 teaspoon vanilla extract
Cream, optional

In a saucepan, combine brown sugar, 1/4 cup flour and 1/4 teaspoon salt. Add water and lemon juice; cook over low heat until thick. Cover and set aside. In a mixing bowl, combine baking powder and remaining flour and salt. Cut in 3 tablespoons butter. Add the milk and mix just until moistened (a few lumps will remain); set aside. Arrange apples in a 9-in. square baking dish; sprinkle with cinnamon. Add nutmeg, vanilla and remaining butter to sauce; pour over apples. Drop dough by spoonfuls over sauce. Bake at 350° for 55 minutes or until top is brown and apples are tender. Serve warm with cream if desired. **Yield:** 9 servings.

CINNAMON SWIRL KUCHEN
Nancy Brown, Janesville, Wisconsin
(PICTURED ON PAGE 37)

This is an old family recipe that we love to serve for breakfast or brunch. It's moist and keeps well, so you can make it a day ahead.

      1/2 cup butter *or* margarine
      1/2 cup shortening
2-1/3 cups sugar, *divided*
        4 eggs
        1 cup milk
        2 teaspoons vanilla extract
        3 cups all-purpose flour
        3 teaspoons baking powder
        1 teaspoon salt
        2 tablespoons ground cinnamon

In a large mixing bowl, cream butter and shortening. Gradually add 2 cups sugar; cream until fluffy. Add eggs, one at a time, beating well after each addition. Combine milk and vanilla; set aside. Sift together flour, baking powder and salt; add to creamed mixture alternately with milk mixture, beating just enough after each addition to keep batter smooth. Combine cinnamon and remaining sugar; sprinkle 1-1/2 teaspoons into a greased 10-in. tube pan. Pour 1/3 of batter into pan. Sprinkle half of remaining cinnamon/sugar; top with 1/3 of batter. Repeat with remaining cinnamon/sugar and batter. Smooth top with spatula. Bake at 350° for 1 hour and 15 minutes. Cool 10 minutes; remove from pan to a wire rack to cool thoroughly. **Yield:** 16-20 servings.

BLACK RASPBERRY DUMPLINGS
Jeanette Redman, Newark, Ohio

These scrumptious dumplings are very easy to fix. I like to prepare them just before a meal and then set them aside to be served warm for dessert. They're good cold, too!

        1 quart fresh *or* frozen black raspberries
1-1/4 cups sugar, *divided*
        1 cup water
        3 tablespoons cornstarch
        3 cups prepared biscuit mix
        1 cup milk
Additional sugar, optional
Ground nutmeg, optional

In a 6-qt. saucepan, combine raspberries, 1 cup sugar, water and cornstarch; stir to blend. Bring to a boil, stirring often. Reduce heat to low. Meanwhile, combine biscuit mix, milk and remaining sugar in a mixing bowl. Mix until a soft dough forms. Drop dough by spoonfuls onto berries. Cook over low heat, uncovered, for 10 minutes. Cover and cook 10-15 minutes more or until dumplings are cooked through. For a glazed effect, sprinkle dumplings with sugar and a dash of nutmeg before serving. **Yield:** 10 servings.

> **EASTER BREAKFAST.** On opposite page: Cinnamon Swirl Kuchen (recipe above).

ALMOND/APRICOT COFFEE CAKE
Sherrie Wakefield, Wickliffe, Kentucky
(PICTURED ON PAGE 40)

This is my favorite family recipe. The almonds and apricots make it a colorful coffee cake and an outstanding dessert.

        1 cup butter, softened
    1-1/2 cups sugar
        3 eggs
        1 cup (8 ounces) sour cream
    3/4 to 1 teaspoon almond extract
        2 cups all-purpose flour
        1 teaspoon baking powder
    1/4 teaspoon salt
    3/4 cup sliced almonds, *divided*
        1 jar (12 ounces) apricot preserves, *divided*

In a large mixing bowl, cream butter and sugar. Add eggs, one at a time, beating well after each addition until smooth and fluffy. On low speed of mixer, blend in sour cream and extract. Combine flour, baking powder and salt; add to creamed mixture and mix just until combined. Sprinkle half of almonds in a greased and floured 10-in. tube pan. Spread half of batter over nuts. Carefully spoon half of preserves over batter, keeping preserves away from edges of pan. Sprinkle with remaining almonds. Spoon on remaining batter; add remaining preserves to center of batter. Bake at 350° for 50-60 minutes. Cool in pan on rack for 20 minutes. Remove from pan; cool completely. **Yield:** 16 servings.

ROSE'S APPLE TURNOVER COFFEE CAKE
Anne Frederick, New Hartford, New York

Every Saturday our family would go to Grandma Rose's house for a great home-cooked meal. Best of all, though, were the treats she'd send over midweek—especially her homemade turnovers. She never followed a recipe, but this dessert comes very close.

FILLING:
    1/3 cup butter *or* margarine
        4 baking apples, pared and sliced 1/2 inch thick
    3/4 cup sugar
        1 teaspoon grated lemon peel
    1/2 teaspoon ground cinnamon
    1/8 teaspoon ground mace
    1/3 cup currants
DOUGH:
    2-1/2 cups all-purpose flour, *divided*
        3 tablespoons sugar
    1/2 teaspoon salt
        1 package (1/4 ounce) active dry yeast
    3/4 cup water
    1/3 cup butter *or* margarine
        1 egg
        1 teaspoon grated lemon peel
TOPPING:
    3/4 cup chopped pecans
        6 tablespoons all-purpose flour
    1/4 cup confectioners' sugar

        3 tablespoons butter *or* margarine, melted
    1/4 teaspoon ground cinnamon

In a large saucepan, melt butter over medium heat. Add apples and cook, stirring, about 8 minutes or until just tender. Stir in remaining filling ingredients. Cook 10-15 minutes, stirring until thickened. Remove from heat; cool. For dough, in a large mixing bowl, combine 1 cup flour, sugar, salt and yeast. In a small saucepan, combine water and butter; heat on low until temperature reaches 120°. Gradually add to dry ingredients; beat 2 minutes. Beat in egg, peel and 3/4 cup flour. With mixer at high speed, beat 2 minutes. Stir in remaining flour. Cover; let stand 20 minutes. Meanwhile, combine topping ingredients in a small bowl and blend well; set aside. Divide dough in half. On a well-floured surface and using a floured rolling pin, roll each half to a 14-in. x 12-in. rectangle. Place on greased baking sheets. Spread filling down center of dough to within 1 in. of ends. Starting about 3/4 in. from filling, cut 1-in.-wide strips diagonally from filling to edges of dough. Alternately fold opposite strips of dough at angles across filling. Fold ends over filling. Loosely cover dough with greased waxed paper; cover paper with plastic wrap. Refrigerate at least 2 hours. When ready to bake, uncover and let stand at room temperature for 10 minutes. Sprinkle topping over coffee cakes. Bake at 375° for 30-35 minutes or until lightly browned. Remove from baking sheets to wire racks to cool. **Yield:** 2 coffee cakes (16-20 servings).

CHERRY CINNAMON COBBLER
Connie Brueggeman, Sparta, Wisconsin

My mom made this recipe when I was very young. Its cheery color and cinnamon scent make it just right for gray, winter days.

        1 can (16 ounces) pitted tart red cherries
    1/2 cup sugar
        2 to 4 tablespoons red cinnamon candies
        2 tablespoons cornstarch
    1/2 cup water
    1-1/2 cups all-purpose flour
        2 teaspoons baking powder
    1/2 teaspoon salt
        6 tablespoons brown sugar, *divided*
    1/3 cup chopped nuts
    1/4 cup shortening
        1 egg, beaten
        2 tablespoons milk
        1 tablespoon butter
    1/4 teaspoon ground cinnamon

Drain cherries, reserving juice. In a saucepan, combine sugar, candies and cornstarch. Stir in water and juice. Cook over medium heat, stirring occasionally, until thickened. Stir in cherries. Pour into an 8-in. square baking pan; set aside. In a mixing bowl, combine flour, baking powder, salt, 3 tablespoons brown sugar and nuts. Cut in shortening until crumbly. Add egg and milk; mix until dry ingredients are moistened (add a few drops more milk if necessary). Roll out dough; brush with butter. Combine cinnamon and remaining brown sugar; sprinkle over dough. Roll up; cut into 16 slices. Lay slices over cherry filling. Bake at 400° for 35-30 minutes. Serve warm. **Yield:** 8 servings.

From Grandma's Kitchen: Cherry Coffee Cake

Heidi Schwanz

"Whenever I serve my grandmother's Cherry Coffee Cake, it always gets rave reviews."

When Heidi Schwanz thinks of her grandmother, she remembers the thick quilts Grandma made for each of her 14 grandchildren, her homemade noodles drying on the backs of chairs, and—best of all—the delicious Cherry Coffee Cake that she made in a giant jelly roll pan.

"I love to bake from scratch using family recipes —especially Grandma's recipe for Cherry Coffee Cake!" she says.

Today, Heidi prepares her grandmother's timeless dessert in the same pan, and has served it to family and friends in her hometown of Chili, Wisconsin and even as far away as Czechoslovakia—sort of!

Heidi will never forget the day two Czechoslovakian chaps, whom she had befriended on a high-school trip overseas, made a surprise visit to her family's farm. Heidi invited the two travelers (who were brothers) to stay for a few days, but had nothing special to serve her foreign friends. So that night, after everyone had gone to bed, she and her mother got busy baking a big batch of Cherry Coffee Cake to serve as a special breakfast treat.

The next morning, when the brothers came into the kitchen and caught sight of the fruity cake, they immediately stopped in their tracks.

"Their eyes grew really wide and they started talk-

ing to each other in Czechoslovakian," Heidi recalls. "We thought something was wrong until they exclaimed in English: 'This looks just like our grandmother used to make in Czechoslovakia!' "

One bite confirmed their feelings. "This *tastes* just like our grandmother used to make!" the brothers announced.

Heidi was thrilled they liked her Cherry Coffee Cake, but not too surprised—that recipe had been *her* first dessert choice for as long as she could remember.

"Our neighbors had a cherry tree, so we always canned cherries and used the juice to make Cherry Coffee Cake," Heidi explains. "But you can also substitute raspberries, blueberries, apples or peaches for the cherries."

These days, Heidi—a pastor's wife in West Bend, Iowa—gets help from her eager 4-year-old son and 2-year-old twin boys when she makes the dessert.

"They stand at the counter on chairs as I measure ingredients. Then I let them dump the ingredients in the bowl," she says.

The biggest compliment, she concludes, is when family members and visiting relatives ask for "seconds" and say, "Heidi, this Cherry Coffee Cake tastes just like the kind Grandma used to make!"

CHERRY COFFEE CAKE
(PICTURED ON PAGE 40)

> **2 cups all-purpose flour**
> **3 teaspoons baking powder**
> **1 teaspoon salt**
> **1/2 cup sugar**
> **2/3 cup shortening**
> **3/4 cup milk**
> **FILLING:**
> **1 cup sugar *or* sugar to taste**
> **1/4 cup cornstarch**
> **1/4 teaspoon salt**
> **2 cans (16 ounces *each*) pitted tart red cherries**
> **1/4 to 1/2 teaspoon almond extract**
> **Few drops red food coloring, optional**
> **TOPPING:**
> **1/2 cup sugar**
> **1/2 cup all-purpose flour**
> **1-1/2 teaspoons ground cinnamon**
> **1/4 cup butter**

Sift together flour, baking powder, salt and sugar. Place in a large mixing bowl; work in lard. Add milk. Spread into a greased 13-in. x 9-in. x 2-in. baking pan; set aside. For filling, combine sugar, cornstarch and salt in a saucepan. Drain cherries, reserving juice. Set cherries aside and add juice to saucepan. Cook and stir over medium heat until thickened and bubbly; cook and stir 2 minutes more. Remove from heat; stir in extract, and food coloring if desired. Stir in cherries; cool slightly. Spread on dough. For topping, combine sugar, flour and cinnamon in a small bowl. Cut in butter until crumbly; sprinkle over filling. Bake at 350° for 50-55 minutes, or until bubbly and cake tests done. **Yield:** about 20 servings.

RHUBARB COBBLER
Evonne Wurmnest, Normal, Illinois

My mother made this cobbler for hay balers at lunchtime and for her quilt club. I've shared the recipe with many friends and they say it's now one of their favorites!

  3 cups diced rhubarb
  2 cups sugar, *divided*
  1 tablespoon butter *or* margarine
  1/2 cup shortening
  1 egg
  1 cup all-purpose flour
  1 teaspoon baking powder
  1/2 cup milk
Whipped cream *or* ice cream, optional

Place rhubarb in a 13-in. x 9-in. x 2-in. baking pan. Sprinkle 1 cup sugar over and dot with butter. In a mixing bowl, cream shortening and remaining sugar. Beat in egg. Sift together flour and baking powder; add alternately with milk to creamed mixture. Drop by tablespoonfuls over rhubarb. Bake at 350° for 55-60 minutes. Serve warm with whipped cream or ice cream if desired. **Yield:** 10-12 servings. **Variation:** Cherries, peaches or apricots can be substituted for the rhubarb.

OLD-FASHIONED GERMAN COFFEE CAKE
Rev. Willis Piepenbrink, Oshkosh, Wisconsin
(PICTURED ON PAGE 40)

My mom served this moist coffee cake every Sunday after church, but the peach topping was reserved for special occasions, like when company came. Usually, she simply sprinkled sugar and cinnamon on top.

  2 packages (5/8 ounce *each*) compressed yeast cake, crumbled
  1 tablespoon sugar
  1/2 cup warm water (80°-90°)
  1/3 cup shortening, melted
  1/2 cup sugar
  1 egg, beaten
  3-1/2 to 4 cups all-purpose flour, *divided*
  1/2 cup warm milk (80°-90°)
TOPPING:
  1 cup all-purpose flour
  1/2 cup packed brown sugar
  1/2 cup sugar
  1/4 cup shortening
  2 teaspoons vanilla extract
Pinch salt
  2 cans (16 ounces *each*) sliced peaches in syrup, drained

Dissolve yeast and 1 tablespoon sugar in water; let stand 5

COFFEE-KLATCH CLASSICS. On opposite page, top to bottom: Almond/Apricot Coffee Cake (p. 38), Old-Fashioned German Coffee Cake (above), Cherry Coffee Cake (p. 39).

---

minutes. In a large mixing bowl, combine shortening, sugar and egg. Gradually mix in 2 cups flour, milk and yeast mixture. Add enough remaining flour to form a soft dough. Turn out onto a floured surface; knead until smooth and elastic, about 6-8 minutes. Place dough in a greased bowl, turning to grease top. Cover and let rise in a warm place until doubled, about 1 hour. Punch dough down. Divide in half; press each half into a greased 11-in. x 7-in. baking pan. Cover and let rise until doubled, about 1 hour. For topping, combine flour, sugars, shortening, vanilla and salt; sprinkle over dough. Arrange peaches on top. Bake at 375° for 25-30 minutes or until golden brown. **Yield:** 2 coffee cakes (about 20 servings).

CHERRY GRUNT
Judy Meikle, Cherokee, Iowa

My husband and two sons really enjoy this old-time dessert. Besides cooking for them, I'm a hot lunch cook and prepare the main dish for about 1,300 students!

  1 can (16 ounces) pitted tart red cherries, undrained
1-1/2 cups water
  3/4 cup sugar, *divided*
  1/4 cup butter *or* margarine, *divided*
  1 cup all-purpose flour
1-1/2 teaspoons baking powder
Pinch salt
  1/3 cup milk
  1/2 teaspoon vanilla extract

Place cherries and juice in a large saucepan or Dutch oven along with water, 1/2 cup sugar and 2 tablespoons butter. Simmer for 5 minutes. Meanwhile, sift together flour, baking powder, salt and remaining sugar; place in a mixing bowl. Cut in remaining butter with a pastry blender. Add milk and vanilla. Drop by teaspoonfuls over cherry mixture; cover and simmer for 20 minutes. **Yield:** 8-10 servings.

APPLE FRITTERS
Katie Beechy, Seymour, Missouri

Our children ask for fritters each fall when there are plenty of apples available.

2-1/2 cups all-purpose flour
  2 teaspoons baking powder
  1 teaspoon salt
  1/2 cup nonfat dry milk
  1/3 cup sugar
  2 eggs
  1 cup water
  2 cups chopped pared apples
Cooking oil
Sugar

In a mixing bowl, combine first five ingredients. Lightly beat eggs with water; add to dry ingredients and stir just until moistened. Fold in apples. In a skillet, heat oil to 375°. Drop batter by teaspoonfuls into oil and fry until golden brown. Drain on paper towels. Roll in sugar. Serve warm. **Yield:** 40 fritters.

BLACKBERRY COBBLER
Trudy Cinque, Waynesville, North Carolina

My grandmother made this cobbler when I was a little girl. I can still remember the fun we had first picking black-berries together in the hills. Blackberries are my favorite filling, but this cobbler can also be made with apples.

    1 cup butter *or* margarine, *divided*
    1 cup sugar
    1 cup water
1-1/2 cups self-rising flour*
    1/3 cup milk, room temperature
    2 cups fresh *or* frozen blackberries
    1/2 to 1 teaspoon ground cinnamon
    2 tablespoons sugar

In a 10-in. round or oval baking dish, melt 1/2 cup butter; set aside. In a saucepan, heat sugar and water until sugar melts; set aside. Place flour in a mixing bowl; cut in remaining butter until fine crumbs form. Add milk, stirring with a fork until dough leaves sides of bowl. Turn out onto a floured board; knead three or four times. Roll out to an 11-in. x 9-in. rectangle 1/4 in. thick. Spread berries over dough; sprinkle with cinnamon. Roll up, jelly-roll style. Cut into 1/4-in.-thick slices. Carefully lay slices in baking dish over butter. Pour sugar syrup around slices (syrup will be absorbed). Bake at 350° for 45 minutes. Sprinkle sugar over top and bake 15 minutes more. Serve warm or cold. (*If self-rising flour is not available, use 1-1/2 cups all-purpose flour plus 1/4 teaspoon salt and 2-1/4 teaspoons baking powder.) **Yield:** 8 servings.

GRANDMA'S APPLE DUMPLINGS
Janice Thompson, Martin, Michigan

The aroma of these melt-in-your-mouth dumplings re-minds me of my grandma's old-fashioned kitchen. All of her cooking and baking was wonderful!

SAUCE:
1-1/2 cups sugar
1-1/2 cups water
    1/4 cup red cinnamon candies
    1/4 teaspoon ground cinnamon
    1/4 teaspoon ground nutmeg
DUMPLINGS:
    2 cups all-purpose flour
    2 teaspoons baking powder
    1 teaspoon salt
    2/3 cup shortening
    2/3 cup cold milk
    6 small baking apples, peeled and cored
    3 tablespoons butter *or* margarine
    1 egg white, beaten
    1 tablespoon sugar
Half-and-half cream, optional

Combine all sauce ingredients in a medium saucepan. Bring to a full rolling boil, stirring occasionally. Set aside. For dumplings, combine flour, baking powder and salt in a large mixing bowl. Using a fork or pastry blender, cut in shortening until mixture resembles coarse crumbs. Sprinkle in milk, mixing lightly with a fork until a soft dough forms. Shape into a ball. On a lightly floured surface, roll dough

to an 18-in. x 12-in. rectangle. Cut into six squares. Place an apple in the center of each square; dot with butter. Bring corners of pastry up to top of apple; press edges to seal. Place in an ungreased 13-in. x 9-in. x 2-in. baking dish. Pour sauce into pan around dumplings. Brush dumplings with egg white and sprinkle with sugar. Bake at 375° for 50 minutes or until light golden brown and apples are tender. Serve warm with cream if desired. **Yield:** 6 servings.

> **OUT OF BROWN SUGAR?** Substitute 2 tablespoons molasses and 1/2 cup granulated sugar for every 1/2 cup of brown sugar called for. (Add the molasses to the batter with the other liquid ingredients.)

IVA'S PEACH COBBLER
Ruby Ewart, Boise, Idaho

My mother received this recipe from a friend of hers many years ago, and fortunately she shared it with me. Boise is situated right between two large fruit-producing areas in our state, so peaches are plentiful in the summer.

    6 to 8 large ripe peaches, peeled and sliced
2-1/2 tablespoons cornstarch
    3/4 to 1 cup sugar
CRUST:
    1 cup all-purpose flour
    2 egg yolks
    1/4 cup butter *or* margarine, melted
    1 teaspoon baking powder
    1 cup sugar
    2 egg whites, stiffly beaten

Combine peaches, cornstarch and sugar; place in a greased 13-in. x 9-in. x 2-in. baking dish. For crust, combine flour, egg yolks, butter, baking powder and sugar in a mixing bowl. Gently fold in egg whites. Spread over peaches. Bake at 375° for about 45 minutes or until the fruit is bubbling around edges and the top is golden. **Yield:** 12 servings.

RHUBARB PINWHEEL DUMPLINGS
Patricia Habiger, Spearville, Kansas

This recipe's rich, buttery biscuit dough, covered with chopped rhubarb and rolled like a jelly roll, is heavenly baked in sheer pink cinnamon sauce.

SAUCE:
1-1/2 cups sugar
    1 tablespoon all-purpose flour
    1/4 teaspoon ground cinnamon
    1/4 teaspoon salt
1-1/2 cups water
    1/3 cup butter
    1 teaspoon vanilla extract
Few drops red food coloring, optional
DUMPLINGS:
    2 cups all-purpose flour

2 tablespoons sugar
2 teaspoons baking powder
1/4 teaspoon salt
2-1/2 tablespoons cold butter
1/2 to 3/4 cup milk
FILLING:
2 tablespoons butter, softened
2 cups finely chopped fresh *or* frozen rhubarb
1/2 cup sugar
1/2 teaspoon ground cinnamon
Cream, optional

In a small saucepan, combine sugar, flour, cinnamon and salt. Gradually mix in water; add butter. Bring to a boil over high heat and cook for 1 minute. Remove from heat; add vanilla. If desired, add enough food coloring to turn the mixture a deep pink. Let cool. For dumplings, combine flour, sugar, baking powder and salt in a medium mixing bowl. Cut in butter until mixture resembles small peas. Add milk and mix quickly but do not overmix. Shape dough into a ball. On a floured surface, roll dough to a 12-in. x 10-in. rectangle. Spread dough with butter and arrange rhubarb on top. Sprinkle sugar and cinnamon over all. Roll up, jelly-roll style, starting at a long end. Cut into 12 slices. Arrange, cut side up, in a greased 3-qt. baking dish. Pour sauce over dumplings. Bake at 350° for 35 minutes or until dumplings are puffy and golden brown. Serve warm with cream if desired. **Yield:** 12 servings.

APRICOT KUCHEN
Ellen Ebbersten, Elkhart, Illinois

A neighbor gave me this recipe in 1927 when I was just a new bride. It's spiced with cardamom and tastes luscious!

8 ounces dried apricot halves
3 cups cold water
2 cups sugar
4 cups all-purpose flour
1 cup butter
1 package (1/4 ounce) active dry yeast
1 cup warm water (110°-115°)
1/4 cup sugar
1 teaspoon salt
3 eggs, beaten
1 teaspoon ground cardamom
Ground cinnamon
Additional sugar

Place apricots and water in a bowl; soak overnight. In a saucepan, place apricots, soaking liquid and sugar. Simmer until apricots are transparent. Cool; drain and set aside. Place flour in a mixing bowl; cut in butter until mixture resembles coarse crumbs. Dissolve yeast in water; add to crumb mixture along with sugar, salt, eggs and cardamom. Beat until smooth (dough will be soft and sticky). Place dough in a greased bowl, turning once to grease top. Cover and let rise in a warm place until doubled, about 1-1/2 hours. On a floured surface or pastry cloth, knead dough for 2 minutes. Divide into three portions; roll each in a 9-in. circle. Place each in a greased 9-in. round cake pan. Let rise until doubled, about 1-1/4 hours. Place apricots on top of dough. Combine cinnamon and sugar; sprinkle over apricots. Bake at 350° for 25-30 minutes. Cool on wire racks. **Yield:** 3 kuchens (about 24 servings).

FRUIT KUCHEN
Connie Meiselwitz, Kiel, Wisconsin

This German recipe—passed down by my grandma—is one of the first desserts I made when I was young. Now I remember patting the crust into the pan many times. Now I work at a bakery but still make it often, especially in the summer when fresh fruit is plentiful.

CRUST:
1-1/2 cups all-purpose flour
1/2 teaspoon salt
1 tablespoon sugar
1/2 cup butter *or* margarine
1 egg, beaten
1 tablespoon milk
FILLING:
4 to 6 cups fresh fruit (quartered apples, peaches, plums, etc.)
1 cup sugar
1 tablespoon all-purpose flour
2 eggs, beaten
1 cup cream
1/2 teaspoon vanilla extract
CRUMB TOPPING:
1/2 cup sugar
1/2 cup all-purpose flour
2 tablespoons butter *or* margarine, softened

In a mixing bowl, combine flour, salt and sugar; cut in butter until mixture resembles cornmeal. Mix egg and milk; add to flour mixture. Pat into a greased 13-in. x 9-in. x 2-in. baking pan. Arrange fruit on crust. Combine remaining filling ingredients; pour over fruit. For topping, combine ingredients until crumbly; sprinkle over filling. Bake at 350° for 50-60 minutes. **Yield:** 12-15 servings.

ZUCCHINI "APPLE" CRISP
Sherry Hagemann, Ashton, Illinois

I was delightfully surprised to find that a squash could taste identical to a fruit. What's more, this crisp is delicious!

8 cups sliced zucchini (cut like apple slices)
3/4 cup lemon juice
1 teaspoon ground nutmeg
1/2 cup sugar
2 teaspoons ground cinnamon
TOPPING:
1-1/3 cups packed brown sugar
1 cup all-purpose flour
1 cup rolled oats
2/3 cup butter, softened
Whipped cream *or* ice cream, optional

Place zucchini and lemon juice in a large saucepan. Cover and cook over medium heat, stirring occasionally, until zucchini is tender, about 15 minutes. Add nutmeg, sugar and cinnamon; blend until sugar dissolves. Remove from the heat. Pour into a greased 13-in. x 9-in. x 2-in. baking pan. For topping, combine brown sugar, flour, oats and butter until crumbly. Sprinkle over zucchini. Bake at 375° for 50 minutes or until topping is golden brown. Serve warm with whipped cream or ice cream if desired. **Yield:** 12-16 servings.

Cookies & Bars

REMEMBER your grandmother's "cooky jar"? When you reached inside, you could always count on it being filled with hidden treasures—cookies studded with raisins or currants, crunchy with nuts or oats, or fragrant with anise, cinnamon and other spices.

A plate of those sweet-and-satisfying treats, along with a glass of cold milk or a cup of hot tea, was as comforting as a cozy quilt on a chilly night. But nearly as nice as eating those cookies was watching Grandma make them!

For holidays, she'd use her trusty wooden rolling pin to roll out dough, then create fancy shapes with old-fashioned, floured cutters. At other times, she'd bake a batch of bars or drop spoonfuls of sticky dough on a cake pan turned upside down. The aroma of Grandma's freshly baked cookies caused everyone to swoon with delight.

The following chapter is a "cooky jar" of time-tested recipes passed down and perfected by generations of grandmothers. So reach in and help yourself to a handful of these homey old-time treats... and enjoy the memories.

═♥♥♥═

OREGON'S HAZELNUT CHOCOLATE CHIP COOKIES
Mrs. Selmer Looney, Eugene, Oregon
(PICTURED ON PAGE 44)

Oregon has an abundance of nuts, and these nutty cookies are popular with the ladies at my craft club. Growing up during the Depression, my mother taught us to use what was available and said, "It doesn't have to be expensive to be good." She was right!

    1 cup butter *or* margarine, softened
    1/2 cup sugar
    1 cup packed brown sugar
    2 eggs
    1 teaspoon vanilla extract
2-1/3 cups all-purpose flour
    1 teaspoon baking soda
    1/2 teaspoon salt
    1 cup (6 ounces) chocolate chips
    3/4 cup chopped hazelnuts

HOMEMADE HAPPINESS. Opposite page, top to bottom: Oregon's Hazelnut Chocolate Chip Cookies, Peanut Butter Cookies (both recipes above), Raisin-Filled Cookies (p. 46).

In a large mixing bowl, cream butter and sugars on medium speed for 3 minutes. Add eggs, one at a time, beating well after each addition, and vanilla. Combine flour, baking soda and salt; add gradually to batter along with chips and nuts. Drop by heaping tablespoonfuls 3 in. apart onto lightly greased baking sheets. Flatten with a fork. Bake at 375° for 10-12 minutes or until light brown. Remove to a wire rack to cool **Yield:** 3 dozen.

═♥♥♥═

PEANUT BUTTER COOKIES
Janet Hall, Clinton, Wisconsin
(PICTURED ON PAGE 44)

My mother insisted that my grandmother write down one recipe for her when she got married in 1942. That was a real effort because Grandma was a traditional pioneer-type cook who used "a little of this or that 'til it feels right". This treasured recipe is the only one she ever wrote down!

    1 cup shortening
    1 cup peanut butter
    1 cup sugar
    1 cup packed brown sugar
    3 eggs
    3 cups all-purpose flour
    2 teaspoons baking soda
1/4 teaspoon salt

In a mixing bowl, cream shortening, peanut butter and sugars. Add eggs, one at a time, beating well after each addition. Sift together flour, baking soda and salt; add to creamed mixture. Roll into 1-1/2-in. balls and place 3 in. apart on ungreased cookie sheets. Flatten with a fork if desired. Bake at 375° for 10-15 minutes. **Yield:** 3-4 dozen.

═♥♥♥═

GINGER BISCUITS
Mrs. Racine Rockwood, South Weymouth, Massachusetts

My English cousin in Yorkshire sent me this old-fashioned recipe for buttery ginger cookies (or "biscuits" if you're British). You'll love the taste!

2-1/2 cups biscuit mix *or* self-rising flour
    1/2 cup sugar
1-1/4 to 1-1/2 teaspoons ground ginger
    1 teaspoon baking soda
Pinch salt
    1/2 egg, beaten
    1/2 cup corn syrup *or* maple syrup
    4 tablespoons butter

In a mixing bowl, combine biscuit mix or flour, sugar, ginger, soda and salt. Using hands, rub egg into mixture. In a saucepan, warm syrup and butter; stir into batter. Let stand for 3-4 minutes, then knead. Roll heaping teaspoonfuls into small balls. Place 2 in. apart on greased cookie sheets. Bake at 325° for 12-15 minutes. Cookies will flatten and "crackle" when done. **Yield:** 3 dozen.

RAISIN-FILLED COOKIES

Barbara Noel, Junction City, Kansas

(PICTURED ON PAGE 44)

Our family has been making these flavorful cookies for years and years. We love the sweet raisin filling hidden in each cookie.

- 1 cup packed brown sugar
- 1 cup sugar
- 1 cup butter *or* margarine, softened
- 3 eggs
- 2 tablespoons vanilla extract
- 5 cups all-purpose flour
- 1 teaspoon baking powder
- 1 teaspoon baking soda
- 1/4 teaspoon ground nutmeg
- 1/2 teaspoon salt
- 3 tablespoons buttermilk

FILLING:

- 1 tablespoon cornstarch
- 3 tablespoons all-purpose flour
- 1 cup packed brown sugar
- 2 cups boiling water
- 1-1/2 cups seedless raisins

In a mixing bowl, cream sugars and butter. Add eggs, beating well after each addition, and vanilla. Combine dry ingredients; add alternately with buttermilk to creamed mixture. Mix well. Chill. For filling, combine cornstarch, flour and brown sugar in a saucepan. Add water, stirring constantly. Add raisins; stir and cook until mixture comes to a boil and is thickened, about 3 minutes. Cool. On a floured surface, roll dough and cut into 3-in. circles. Spoon 2 teaspoons filling on a circle and top with another circle. Pinch edges together and cut slit in top. Repeat with remaining dough and filling. Place on ungreased cookie sheets. Bake at 350° for 10-13 minutes or until lightly browned. **Yield:** about 3-1/2 dozen.

GLAZED APPLE COOKIES

Marietta Saladin, Woodstock, Illinois

I've had this recipe since my first child was little…now it's a favorite of my grandchildren! I like to use Jonathan apples in the recipe, but you can use the apple of your choice.

- 1/2 cup shortening
- 1-1/2 cups packed brown sugar
- 1 teaspoon baking soda
- 1 teaspoon salt
- 1 teaspoon ground cinnamon
- 1 teaspoon ground cloves
- 1/2 teaspoon ground nutmeg
- 1 egg, beaten
- 1 cup finely chopped peeled apples
- 1 cup chopped walnuts
- 1 cup raisins
- 1/4 cup apple juice *or* milk
- 2 cups all-purpose flour, *divided*

VANILLA GLAZE:

- 1-1/2 cups confectioners' sugar
- 1 tablespoon butter *or* margarine
- 1/4 teaspoon vanilla extract

- 1/8 teaspoon salt
- 2-1/2 tablespoons light cream

In a large mixing bowl, combine shortening, sugar, baking soda, spices and egg. Stir in apples, nuts, raisins, juice or milk and half of the flour; mix well. Blend in the remaining flour. Drop by heaping tablespoonfuls onto greased cookie sheets. Bake at 400° for 10-12 minutes. Combine glaze ingredients and frost cookies while warm. **Yield:** about 3 dozen.

GRANDMA'S OATMEAL COOKIES

Mary Ann Konechne, Kimball, South Dakota

This recipe—a favorite of my husband's—goes back to my great-grandmother. At Christmastime, we use colored sugar for a festive touch.

- 2 cups sugar
- 1-1/2 cups shortening
- 2 teaspoons baking soda
- 4 teaspoons warm water
- 4 eggs
- 4 cups all-purpose flour
- 1/2 teaspoon salt
- 2 teaspoons ground cinnamon
- 4 cups quick-cooking oats
- 2 cups chopped raisins
- 1 cup chopped walnuts

Additional granulated sugar *or* colored sugar

In a large mixing bowl, cream sugar and shortening. Dissolve baking soda in water; add to creamed mixture. Add eggs, one at a time, beating well after each addition. Add remaining ingredients except additional sugar; mix well. Roll out dough; sprinkle with sugar or colored sugar. Cut with desired cutters. Place on greased cookie sheets. Bake at 350° for 12-15 minutes. **Yield:** 12 dozen.

HUNGARIAN NUT HORNS

Rosemary Protz, Brea, California

My mother shared this recipe with me over 30 years ago. Nut horns are especially nice for buffets because they are easy to pick up and eat with your fingers. They also freeze well.

- 1 package (1/4 ounce) active dry yeast
- 1/4 cup warm water (110°-115°)
- 4 cups all-purpose flour
- 1/2 teaspoon salt
- 1-1/2 cups butter
- 3 egg yolks, lightly beaten
- 1/4 cup sour cream
- 1 teaspoon vanilla extract

Confectioners' sugar

NUT FILLING:

- 3 egg whites
- 1 cup sugar
- 1-1/2 cups ground walnuts
- 1 teaspoon vanilla extract

Dissolve yeast in water; set aside. In a large bowl, combine flour and salt. Cut in butter with pastry blender or hands. Add egg yolks, sour cream and vanilla. Mix well with hands (dough will not be sticky). For filling, beat egg whites until very stiff but not dry. Gradually add sugar and continue beating until stiff. Fold in walnuts and vanilla. Divide dough into eight parts. On a pastry cloth heavily covered with confectioners' sugar, roll one part into a 12-in.-diameter circle. Cut into 12 wedges. Spread 1 teaspoon filling on each wedge; tuck in edges of wide end and roll up toward narrow point. Repeat with remaining dough and filling, replenishing confectioners' sugar on pastry cloth to prevent sticking. Place on parchment paper-lined cookie sheets. Bake at 375° for 12-14 minutes or until very light brown. **Yield:** 8 dozen.

When you were a child,
Did your heart skip a beat
When a sweet aroma signaled a treat?
There's nothing like homemade cookies and cake
Just like Grandma used to bake!

RAISIN SHEET COOKIES
Beverly Plymell, Keytesville, Missouri

Looking for a quick sheet cookie for crowds? This delicately spiced, moist variation is kid-tested...and grandkid-tested!

1 cup raisins
1-1/4 cups water
1 cup shortening
1-1/2 cups sugar
2 eggs
1-1/2 teaspoons baking soda
3 cups all-purpose flour
1/4 teaspoon ground nutmeg
1/4 teaspoon ground cinnamon
1/2 teaspoon salt
1 cup chopped nuts
Confectioners' sugar icing, optional

In a small saucepan, combine raisins and water; bring to a boil. Drain; reserve 1 cup liquid and set raisins aside. In a mixing bowl, cream shortening and sugar; add eggs. Add baking soda to raisin liquid. Sift together flour, nutmeg, cinnamon and salt; add alternately with raisin liquid to creamed mixture. Stir in raisins and nuts. Spread in a lightly greased 15-in. x 10-in. x 1-in. baking pan. Bake at 350° for 25-30 minutes. If desired, glaze with confectioners' sugar icing while hot. Cut while warm. **Yield:** 5-6 dozen.

PEANUT CHOCOLATE CHIP COOKIES
Jodie McCoy, Tulsa, Oklahoma

The peanutty taste makes this cookie a real family pleaser.

1 cup butter *or* margarine, softened
1 cup sugar
1 cup packed brown sugar
2 eggs
1 teaspoon vanilla extract
1 cup creamy peanut butter
2 cups all-purpose flour
2 teaspoons baking powder
1/2 teaspoon salt
1 cup Spanish peanuts
1 cup (6 ounces) chocolate chips

In a large mixing bowl, cream butter and sugars. Add eggs, one at a time, beating well after each addition. Add vanilla; beat until fluffy. Blend in peanut butter. Combine dry ingredients; gradually add to batter. Stir in peanuts and chips. Drop by teaspoonfuls onto greased cookie sheets. Bake at 350° for about 8 minutes. **Yield:** 7-8 dozen.

NO-BAKE CORNFLAKE COOKIES
Denise Marnell, Hereford, Texas

I grew up on a farm where we hand-milked cows and had plenty of milk and cream to use for cooking. Sometimes we'd substitute light cream for the evaporated milk in this recipe. We'd rarely let these cookies cool before sampling them, and a batch never lasted a day!

4 cups cornflakes
1-1/2 cups flaked coconut
3/4 cup chopped pecans
1/2 cup light corn syrup
1-1/2 cups sugar
Dash salt
1/2 cup evaporated milk
1/4 cup butter

In a large bowl, combine cornflakes, coconut and pecans; set aside. Place remaining ingredients in a 1-qt. saucepan. Bring mixture to 240° (soft-ball stage), stirring constantly. Add syrup mixture to dry ingredients; stir well. Drop by tablespoonfuls onto waxed paper. Cool. **Yield:** 3-4 dozen.

FUDGE BROWNIES
Becky Albright, Norwalk, Ohio
(PICTURED ON OUR COVER)

There's no brownie recipe or mix I've ever tried that's better than this! It's so easy besides—you can mix it in one bowl in just a few minutes. My husband's grandmother passed the recipe on; now our son makes these brownies for after-school snacks.

1-1/3 cups all-purpose flour
2 cups sugar
3/4 cup baking cocoa
1 teaspoon baking powder
1/2 teaspoon salt
1/2 cup chopped nuts
2/3 cup vegetable oil
4 eggs, lightly beaten
2 teaspoons vanilla extract
1 cup chopped nuts, optional

In a mixing bowl, combine first six ingredients. In another bowl, combine oil, eggs and vanilla; add to dry ingredients. Do not overmix. Spread in a 13-in. x 9-in. x 2-in. baking pan. Sprinkle with nuts if desired. Bake at 350° for 20-25 minutes or until toothpick inserted in center comes out clean. **Yield:** about 2 dozen.

GRANDMA BRUBAKER'S ORANGE COOKIES

Sheri DeBolt, Huntington, Indiana

At least two generations of my family have enjoyed the recipe for these light, delicate, orange-flavored cookies.

    1 cup shortening
    2 cups sugar
    2 eggs, *separated*
    1 cup sour milk*
    5 cups all-purpose flour
    2 teaspoons baking powder
    2 teaspoons baking soda
Pinch salt
Juice and peel of 2 medium oranges
ICING:
    2 cups confectioners' sugar
    1/4 cup orange juice
    1 tablespoon butter *or* margarine
    1 tablespoon grated orange peel

In a mixing bowl, cream shortening and sugar. Beat in egg yolks and milk. Sift together flour, baking powder, soda and salt; add alternately with orange juice and peel to creamed mixture. Add egg whites and beat until smooth. Drop by rounded teaspoonfuls onto greased cookie sheets. Bake at 325° for 10 minutes. For icing, combine all ingredients and beat until smooth. Frost cookies when cool. **Yield:** about 6 dozen. (*To sour milk, place 1 tablespoon white vinegar in a measuring cup; add enough milk to equal 1 cup.)

CHOCOLATE BUTTERMILK BROWNIES

Clarice Baker, Stromsburg, Nebraska

I've made these frosted brownies for so many years, I don't need a recipe card to follow. When our three grandchildren visit the farm, they're delighted when I serve these—plain or with ice cream.

    1 cup butter *or* margarine
    1/4 cup unsweetened cocoa
    1 cup water
    2 cups sugar
    2 cups all-purpose flour
    1/2 teaspoon salt
    1/2 cup buttermilk
    1 teaspoon baking soda
    2 eggs, beaten
    1 teaspoon vanilla extract
    3 to 4 drops red food coloring, optional
FROSTING:
    1/2 cup butter *or* margarine
    1/4 cup unsweetened cocoa
    1/4 cup buttermilk
    1 pound confectioners' sugar
    1 teaspoon vanilla extract
Dash salt
    3/4 cup chopped almonds, optional

In a saucepan, bring butter, cocoa and water to a boil. Cool. Meanwhile, in a large mixing bowl, combine sugar, flour and salt. Pour cocoa mixture over dry ingredients; mix well. Combine buttermilk and baking soda; add to batter along with eggs, vanilla, and food coloring if desired. Mix until well combined. Pour into a greased 15-in. x 10-in. x 1-in. greased and floured baking pan. Bake at 350° for 20 minutes. For frosting, melt butter, cocoa and buttermilk in a saucepan. Stir in sugar, vanilla and salt. Spread over warm cake. Top with nuts if desired. **Yield:** 15 brownies.

GREAT-AUNT AMY'S DATE BARS

Pamela Kinney, Irving, Texas

This recipe has been handed down from my Great-Aunt Amy, who was born in 1879. My mother baked these bars every Christmas, and now my sisters and I bake them for our own family holiday gatherings.

    1 package (8 ounces) pitted dates, chopped, *divided*
    1 cup plus 1 tablespoon all-purpose flour, *divided*
    3 eggs, well beaten
    1 cup sugar
    1 teaspoon baking powder
    3 tablespoons milk
    1 cup walnut pieces
Confectioners' sugar

Roll half of the dates in 1 tablespoon flour; arrange in bottom of a greased and floured 9-in. x 9-in. baking pan. In a bowl, combine remaining ingredients except confectioners' sugar; mix well. Spread over dates. Bake at 350° for 40 minutes. Cool; cut into squares and roll in confectioners' sugar. **Yield:** 6-7 dozen.

CHEWY CHOCOLATE COOKIES

Sheri Ziesemer, Olympia, Washington

This cookie recipe—a favorite of our four children—has been in my collection for years. Sometimes I'll substitute mint-flavored chips for the semisweet chocolate ones. Either way, the cookies disappear quickly.

1-1/4 cups butter *or* margarine
    2 cups sugar
    2 eggs
    2 teaspoons vanilla extract
    2 cups all-purpose flour
    3/4 cup unsweetened cocoa
    1 teaspoon baking soda
    1/2 teaspoon salt
    2 cups (12 ounces) semisweet chocolate chips

In a mixing bowl, cream butter and sugar. Add eggs, one at a time, beating well after each addition, and vanilla. Combine dry ingredients; gradually add to creamed mixture. Stir in chips. Drop by teaspoonfuls onto lightly greased cookie sheets. Bake at 350° for 8-10 minutes. Do not overbake. Cool about 1 minute on pans, then remove to wire racks. **Yield:** about 4-1/2 dozen.

CHIP TIP: For spicy-good chocolate chip cookies, add 1 teaspoon ground cinnamon to the batter.

FROM GRANDMA'S KITCHEN:
Chewy Date Pinwheels

Naomi Cross

"It seems Grandmas know that cookies always warm a child's heart!"

When school let out each summer, Naomi Cross looked forward to spending time at her Amish grandparents' farm. There she enjoyed the cows, chickens, horses, helping in the garden—especially the daily horse-and-buggy rides with her grandfather. But the best part of her visits? It was baking Chewy Date Pinwheels with her grandma.

"Those cookies were a very important part of each visit!" says Naomi, who grew up with five sisters and brothers just 7 miles from her grandparents' place. "Unlike our parents, Grandma and Grandpa didn't have electricity—or a car or phone, for that matter—so we baked the cookies on a wood-burning stove, which took some doing!"

Naomi's grandmother let the girls take turns stirring the date mixture on the stove. If the mixture got too hot, she'd move it to the back of the stove.

"She also let us spread the dates on the rolled-out dough and later we'd place the cookies on a cookie sheet," Naomi recalls, adding, "Grandma had lots of patience with us!"

Even cleanup time was an adventure. To wash the dishes, they had to take heated water from the stove's reservoir and pour it in the dry sink's dishpan. "Afterward, we tossed the dirty water out an open kitchen window!" she says with a chuckle.

Naomi loved baking with her grandmother and enjoyed her visits most when she had Grandma all to herself. "I miss the good old days of going to see Grandma, but those cookies will always remind me of her kindness to us children."

Naomi continues to make Chewy Date Pinwheels —with a little help from modern conveniences—for her husband and five children on their farm in Goshen, Indiana. "Pinwheels still take a little more time to make than some cookies, but the end result is worth it," she says. "They're a special treat around here."

Although their children are still too young to get very involved in the kitchen—other than eating and helping do the dishes—"they put their fingers in the cookie batter whenever they can!" she says with a grin.

"I really treasure the memories of my grandmother," Naomi adds. "I plan to pass on her kindness—and her cookie recipe—to my children, and grandchildren, too!"

CHEWY DATE PINWHEELS

1-1/2 cups chopped dates
    1 cup sugar
    1 cup water
  1/2 cup chopped pecans
    1 cup butter *or* margarine
    2 cups packed brown sugar
  1/2 cup sugar
    3 eggs
4-1/2 cups all-purpose flour
    1 teaspoon salt
    1 teaspoon baking soda
    1 teaspoon ground cinnamon

In a saucepan, combine dates, sugar and water. Cook over medium heat, stirring constantly, until thick, about 8 minutes. Add nuts; cool. Meanwhile, cream butter and sugars in a mixing bowl. Add eggs, one at a time, beating well after each addition. Combine dry ingredients; add gradually to creamed mixture. Divide dough in half. On a lightly floured surface, roll each half to a 1/4-in.-thick rectangle. Spread each with half the date filling; roll up, jelly-roll style. Wrap with plastic wrap; chill overnight. Cut rolls into 1/2-in. slices. Place 2 in. apart on greased cookie sheets. Bake at 375° for about 12 minutes. Cool on wire racks. **Yield:** about 4 dozen.

CHRISTMAS CHEER. Clockwise from bottom left: Springerle (p. 52), Fruitcake Cookies (p. 52), Spritz Cookies (p. 52), Coffee Bonbons (p. 52), Pecan Puffs (p. 53), Frieda's Molasses Cookies (p. 53), Angel Sugar Crisps (p. 53).

SPRINGERLE
Bonnie Ziolecki, Menomonee Falls, Wisconsin
(PICTURED ON PAGE 50)

*When my husband and I acquired some antique spring-
erle cookie boards from an elderly German couple 20
years ago, we learned some lore to go with them. "Stir the
batter by hand clockwise for 1 hour," they told us. This
signified the passing of time and the channeling of it into
something beautiful and valuable—these cookies!*

    2 eggs
    1 cup sugar
    2 cups all-purpose flour
1/4 teaspoon salt
    1 teaspoon baking powder
    1 teaspoon anise extract *or* anise seed

In a mixing bowl, beat eggs at high speed until thick and
light-colored. Gradually add sugar, beating on low until
dissolved, about 10 minutes. Sift together flour, salt and
baking powder; fold into egg/sugar mixture. Add anise. On
a well-floured board or pastry cloth, place a small portion
of dough. Coat dough with flour and pat with hands to
1/3-in. thickness. Dust springerle rolling pin with flour.
Working quickly, press rolling pin onto dough to emboss
the designs and get a clear imprint. Cut out squares and
place on greased cookie sheets. Repeat with remaining
dough. Allow cookies to dry at room temperature 4-6
hours. Bake at 350° for 10-12 minutes. Cool; store in airtight containers. **Editor's Note:** To soften cookies for eating, place them in a sealed crock with a slice of apple overnight, or dunk them in coffee. **Yield:** about 3 dozen.

Did You Know? Wooden springerle molds first sprang
up in Germany and were usually embossed with designs
of prosperity, such as a farmer carrying wheat, but some
of the earliest designs were religious in nature. Once dry,
the hardened cookies were often decorated for the
Christmas tree. New molds in ceramic or wood can be
purchased in gourmet kitchen shops.

FRUITCAKE COOKIES
Julia Funkhouser, Carson, Iowa
(PICTURED ON PAGE 50)

*As holiday gifts, these rich fruit-and-nut-filled cookies are
pretty and practical—the taste actually improves with age!*

    1 cup butter, softened
3/4 cup packed brown sugar
    1 egg
1/2 teaspoon vanilla extract
1-1/2 cups (rounded) all-purpose flour
1/2 teaspoon salt
1/2 teaspoon baking soda
    4 ounces red candied cherries, halved
    4 ounces candied pineapple, diced
1-1/2 cups dates, finely cut
1/2 cup broken walnuts
1/2 cup broken pecans
1/2 cup whole hazelnuts

In a mixing bowl, cream butter, sugar, egg and vanilla. Sift
together flour, salt and soda; add to creamed mixture. Stir in
fruits and nuts. Drop by teaspoonfuls onto greased cookie
sheets. Bake at 325° for 15 minutes. Store tightly covered;
cookies are best after a few days. **Yield:** 3-1/2 dozen.

SPRITZ COOKIES
Sharon Claussen, Wheat Ridge, Colorado
(PICTURED ON PAGE 50)

*It was a tradition to make these cookies with my grand-
mother every Christmas. Now our two daughters help me
make them for the holidays.*

    1 pound butter (no substitutes)
    1 cup sugar
    2 eggs
    2 teaspoons vanilla extract
    4 cups all-purpose flour
    1 teaspoon baking powder

In a mixing bowl, cream butter and sugar. Add eggs, one
at a time, beating well after each addition, and vanilla.
Combine flour and baking powder; add to creamed mixture and mix well. Shape with a cookie press. Place on
ungreased cookie sheets. Bake at 325° for 12-15 minutes
or until light brown. **Yield:** 11-12 dozen.

*Christmas baking still takes work
As it did years ago.
It still takes nuts and fruit and spice,
A dash of love and dough.
There's only one thing different now
And Grandma says, "My land!"
The electric oven cleans itself
Without a helping hand.*

COFFEE BONBONS
Leitzel Malzahn, Fox Point, Wisconsin
(PICTURED ON PAGE 51)

*When I first sampled this unique cookie, I decided it was
the best cookie I'd ever tasted! The coffee flavor and chocolate icing make it a delightful treat at buffets and church
socials. I plan to share it with my out-of-state granddaughters next time they visit.*

    1 cup butter
3/4 cup confectioners' sugar
1/2 teaspoon vanilla extract
    1 tablespoon instant coffee granules
1-3/4 cups all-purpose flour
CHOCOLATE GLAZE:
    1 tablespoon butter
1/2 ounce unsweetened chocolate
    1 cup confectioners' sugar
    2 tablespoons milk

In a mixing bowl, cream butter and sugar until light and
fluffy. Add vanilla. Combine coffee and flour; stir into
creamed mixture and mix well. Chill. Shape into 3/4-in.

balls and place on ungreased cookie sheets. Bake at 350° for 18-20 minutes. Meanwhile, for glaze, melt butter and chocolate together. Add melted mixture to sugar along with milk; beat until smooth. Frost cookies while still warm. **Yield:** 5 dozen.

―❤❤❤―

FRIEDA'S MOLASSES COOKIES
Nina Sanders, Daly City, California
(PICTURED ON PAGE 51)

During the 1930's and 1940's, neighborhood children would stop on their way home from school to sample my mother's cookies. Dunked in a glass of cold milk, they were a snack that was hard to beat!

      1 cup sugar
      1 cup shortening
      1 cup light molasses *or* sorghum
  1/3 cup boiling water
      1 tablespoon vinegar
      5 cups all-purpose flour
      2 teaspoons baking soda
      1 teaspoon ground ginger
      1 teaspoon ground cinnamon
  1/4 teaspoon salt

In a large bowl, cream sugar and shortening. Add molasses, water and vinegar. Combine flour, baking soda, ginger, cinnamon and salt; beat into creamed mixture. Cover and chill for 3 hours. On a lightly floured board, roll dough to 1/4-in. thickness. Cut with a 2-1/2-in. cutter, drinking glass or decorative cutter dipped in flour. Place on greased baking sheets. Bake at 375° for 8 minutes or until edges are lightly browned. Do not overbake. **Yield:** 6-7 dozen.

―❤❤❤―

FAMILY-FAVORITE SOFT OATMEAL COOKIES
Virginia Bodner, Sandusky, Ohio

My mother got this recipe in about 1910 when she was a housekeeper for the local physician. The doctor's wife was an excellent cook and shared the recipe with my mother, who later shared it with me. Now my five grown children also enjoy baking these cookies for their families—it's a tradition.

      2 cups packed brown sugar
      1 cup shortening
      3 eggs
      3 cups all-purpose flour
      1 teaspoon salt
      1 teaspoon baking powder
      1 teaspoon baking soda
      1 teaspoon ground cinnamon
      1 cup sour milk*
      2 cups rolled oats
      1 cup raisins
      1 cup chopped walnuts

In a large mixing bowl, cream sugar and shortening. Add eggs, one at a time, beating well after each addition. Combine flour, salt, baking powder, soda and cinnamon; add alternately with milk to the creamed mixture. Stir in oats, raisins and nuts. Drop by heaping tablespoonfuls onto greased cookie sheets. Bake at 350° for about 12 minutes or until lightly browned. Remove to a cooling rack. **Yield:** about 5 dozen. (*To sour milk, place 1 tablespoon white vinegar in a measuring cup; add enough milk to equal 1 cup.)

―❤❤❤―

PECAN PUFFS
Leslie Link-Terry, Greendale, Wisconsin
(PICTURED ON PAGE 51)

I just had to share my mom's recipe for these drop cookies. The light-as-a-cloud taste is simply heavenly.

      3 egg whites
  Pinch salt
      1 cup packed brown sugar
  1/2 teaspoon vanilla extract
      1 cup chopped pecans

In a mixing bowl, beat egg whites and salt until soft peaks form. Gradually add sugar, beating until stiff peaks form, about 5-8 minutes. Fold in vanilla and pecans. Drop by well-rounded teaspoonfuls onto greased cookie sheets. Bake at 200° for 50-55 minutes or until firm to the touch. Store in airtight container. **Yield:** 3 dozen.

―❤❤❤―

ANGEL SUGAR CRISPS
Annabel Cox, Olivet, South Dakota
(PICTURED ON PAGE 51)

Whenever I've taken these to church coffees, I've had women come into the kitchen and request the recipe. You'll enjoy this sugar cookie's secret ingredient—brown sugar!

  1/2 cup butter *or* margarine, softened
  1/2 cup shortening
  1/2 cup sugar
  1/2 cup packed brown sugar
      1 egg
      1 teaspoon vanilla extract
      2 cups all-purpose flour
      1 teaspoon baking soda
      1 teaspoon cream of tartar
  1/2 teaspoon salt
  Water
  Additional white *or* colored sugar

In a mixing bowl, cream butter, shortening, sugars, egg and vanilla until light and fluffy. Sift together flour, soda, cream of tartar and salt. Add to creamed mixture; mix until blended. Shape into large marble-size balls. Dip half of ball into water, then in sugar. Place, sugared side up, on ungreased cookie sheets. Bake at 400° for 6 minutes or until done. Cool. **Yield:** 4 dozen.

ANISE COOKIES
Esther Perea, Van Nuys, California

My aunt would make these cookies for dessert. I remember walking into the house and I'd almost swoon when I smelled them baking—the aroma filled every room.

2-1/2 cups all-purpose flour
   3 teaspoons baking powder
1-1/2 teaspoons crushed anise seed
   3/4 teaspoon salt
   1/4 teaspoon ground cinnamon
   1/4 teaspoon ground nutmeg
   1/2 cup butter, softened
   1 cup sugar, *divided*
1-1/4 teaspoons vanilla extract
   2 eggs
   1 cup blanched almonds, toasted and finely
     chopped
   2 teaspoons milk

Combine flour, baking powder, anise seed, salt, cinnamon and nutmeg; set aside. In a separate bowl, cream butter and 3/4 cup sugar until fluffy. Beat in vanilla and eggs. Stir in almonds and flour mixture. Line a baking pan with foil. Divide the dough in half and mold into two 12-in. x 2-in. rectangles on the foil. Smooth the surface of each rectangle, then brush with milk and sprinkle with remaining sugar. Bake at 375° for 20 minutes or until golden brown and firm to the touch. Remove from the oven and reduce heat to 300°. Lift rectangles with foil onto a wire rack; cool 15 minutes. Place rectangles on a cutting board; slice 1/2 in. thick crosswise on the diagonal. Place slices, cut side down, on baking sheets. Bake 10-12 minutes longer. Turn oven off, leaving cookies in oven to cool with door ajar. Store in an airtight container. **Yield:** 3-1/2 dozen.

APPLE CRUMB BARS
Barbara Pickard, Union Lake, Michigan

This has been a favorite recipe of mine for many years. I've made these apple bars for parties and for family, and they're always a hit.

1-1/2 cups packed brown sugar
1-1/2 cups rolled oats
   3 cups all-purpose flour
   3/4 teaspoon baking soda
1-1/4 cups butter *or* margarine, *divided*
   5 to 6 cups thinly sliced pared apples
   1 cup sugar
   3 tablespoons cornstarch
   1 cup boiling water
   1 teaspoon vanilla extract

In a bowl, combine brown sugar, oats, flour, baking soda and 1 cup plus 2 tablespoons butter. Reserve 2 cups for topping; *lightly* pat remaining crumbs into a greased 13-in. x 9-in. x 2-in. baking pan. Arrange apples on top of crumbs; set aside. In a saucepan, combine sugar, cornstarch, water, vanilla and remaining butter. Bring to a boil and cook until thick; spread on apples. Sprinkle reserved crumbs on top. Bake at 350° for 35-45 minutes or until top is lightly browned. **Yield:** 3-4 dozen.

CRUNCHY CHEESECAKE BARS
Sheila Kales, Sceptre, Saskatchewan

Try this lemon-flavored bar when you're looking for something that's not too sweet.

   1 cup all-purpose flour
1/3 cup packed brown sugar
   6 tablespoons butter *or* margarine
   1 package (8 ounces) cream cheese, softened
1/4 cup sugar
   1 egg
   2 tablespoons milk
1/4 teaspoon grated lemon peel
   2 tablespoons lemon juice
1/2 teaspoon vanilla extract
3/4 cup chopped nuts

In a medium bowl, mix flour and brown sugar. Cut in butter until mixture resembles fine crumbs. Set aside 1/2 cup for topping; press remaining crumbs into bottom of ungreased 8-in. x 8-in. x 2-in. baking pan. Bake at 350° for 15 minutes. Meanwhile, in a mixing bowl, beat cream cheese on medium speed for 30 seconds. Add sugar; beat until fluffy. Add egg, milk, lemon peel, juice and vanilla; mix well. Spread over baked crust. Combine nuts with reserved crumbs; sprinkle over cream cheese mixture. Bake 20-25 minutes more or until done. Cool in pan on wire rack. **Yield:** 2 dozen.

SPICY MOLASSES COOKIES
Louann Manning, Lyndonville, New York

I found this family recipe in an old cookbook on a time-worn note, handwritten by my stepdaughter's grandmother. It's a very soft, moist cookie—and tastes great with a big glass of milk.

   1 cup shortening
1-1/2 cups packed brown sugar
   1/4 cup light *or* dark molasses
   3 eggs
3-1/2 cups all-purpose flour
   3 teaspoons ground cinnamon
   1 teaspoon baking soda
1/2 teaspoon salt

1/2 teaspoon ground nutmeg
1/4 teaspoon ground cloves
1/4 teaspoon ground allspice
1 cup chopped walnuts, optional
1 cup raisins, optional

In a large mixing bowl, cream shortening and sugar. Add molasses. Add eggs, one at a time, beating well after each addition. Combine dry ingredients and spices; add to batter and mix lightly. Stir in nuts and raisins if desired; mix well. Drop by teaspoonfuls onto greased cookie sheets. Bake at 350° for 10-12 minutes. **Yield:** about 12 dozen.

―♥♥♥―

SUGARLESS DATE DROPS
Jean Bretz, Williams, Oregon

Notice the nutritious ingredients—and these cookies taste so good, too!

1/2 cup butter *or* margarine, softened
1/2 pound dates, cut up
2 eggs
2 teaspoons vanilla extract
1/4 cup whole wheat flour
1/3 cup dry milk powder
1 cup rolled oats
1/2 cup raisins
1/4 cup carob chips
1/2 cup sunflower seeds
1/2 cup chopped pecans

In a mixing bowl, cream butter. Grind dates; blend with eggs and vanilla to make a paste. Stir into butter. Add remaining ingredients; mix well. Drop by teaspoonfuls 1/2 in. apart on greased cookie sheets. Bake at 325° for 10-15 minutes or until peaks begin to brown. **Yield:** 5 dozen.

―♥♥♥―

SWEET-AS-SUGAR COOKIES
Lorri Hinde, Hillsdale, Wisconsin

I brought these wonderful crunchy cookies to our summer family reunion, and men, women and children alike devoured them...then begged for the recipe!

1 cup butter, softened
1 cup sugar
1 cup confectioners' sugar
1 cup vegetable oil
2 eggs
4-1/4 cups all-purpose flour
1 teaspoon salt
1 teaspoon cream of tartar
1 teaspoon baking soda
1 teaspoon vanilla extract
Additional sugar
Nutmeg

In a mixing bowl, cream butter, sugars and oil. Add eggs, one at a time, beating well after each addition. Add dry ingredients and vanilla; mix well. Refrigerate dough overnight. Form into walnut-size balls and place on greased cookie sheets. Combine sugar and nutmeg; dip glass in mixture and flatten cookies with it. Bake at 375° for 8 minutes. Cool on wire rack. **Yield:** about 5 dozen.

―♥♥♥―

DREAMY FUDGE BAR COOKIES
Loretta Coverdell, Amanda, Ohio

This good-looking, good-tasting bar cookie classic has a hint of almond flavoring.

1 cup shortening
2 cups packed brown sugar
2 eggs
2-1/2 cups all-purpose flour
1 teaspoon baking soda
Dash salt
3 cups rolled oats
CHOCOLATE FILLING:
2 cups (12 ounces) semisweet chocolate chips
1 can (14 ounces) sweetened condensed milk
1 tablespoon butter *or* margarine
1 cup chopped walnuts
1/4 to 1/2 teaspoon almond extract

In a mixing bowl, cream shortening and sugar. Add eggs, one at a time, beating well after each addition. Combine flour, soda, salt and oats; stir into creamed mixture. Set aside. For filling, combine chips, milk and butter in a saucepan. Melt over low heat, stirring until smooth. Cool slightly. Stir in walnuts and extract. Press two-thirds of oatmeal mixture into bottom of a greased 15-in. x 10-in. x 1-in. baking pan. Cover with filling and sprinkle remaining oatmeal mixture on top. Flatten slightly. Bake at 350° for 20 minutes. **Yield:** about 3 dozen.

―♥♥♥―

OATMEAL RAISIN COOKIES
Wendy Coalwell, Abbeville, Georgia

I was given this recipe by a dear friend many years ago. The secret to this cookie recipe is to measure exactly (no guessing on the amounts) and to not overbake.

3 eggs, well beaten
1 teaspoon vanilla extract
1 cup raisins
1 cup shortening
1 cup packed light brown sugar
1 cup sugar
2-1/2 cups all-purpose flour
1 teaspoon salt
2 teaspoons baking soda
2 cups rolled oats
1 cup coarsely chopped pecans, optional

In a large mixing bowl, stir together all ingredients. Shape into 1-in. balls. Place on ungreased baking sheets; flatten with fingers. Bake at 350° for 10-11 minutes or until golden brown. Do not overbake. Remove to a wire rack to cool. **Yield:** about 3-1/2 dozen.

GREAT GARNISH GRATER: An electric salad slicer/shredder works beautifully for grating chocolate garnish directly onto cakes or cookies. A manual vegetable grater also works well.
• To make it easier to grate a chocolate square, first place it in the freezer for about 30 minutes.

CHOCOLATE SNOWBALLS

Dee Derezinski, Waukesha, Wisconsin

(PICTURED ON PAGE 56)

This is my favorite Christmas cookie recipe. The cookies remind me of the snowballs I'd pack as a child during winters here in Wisconsin.

   3/4 cup butter *or* margarine, softened
   1/2 cup sugar
     1 egg
     2 teaspoons vanilla extract
     2 cups all-purpose flour
   1/2 teaspoon salt
     1 cup chopped nuts
     1 cup (6 ounces) chocolate chips
Confectioners' sugar

In a mixing bowl, cream butter and sugar. Add egg and vanilla; mix well. Combine flour and salt; stir into creamed mixture. Fold in nuts and chips. Roll into 1-in. balls. Place on ungreased cookie sheets. Bake at 350° for 15-20 minutes. Cool cookies slightly before rolling them in confectioners' sugar. **Yield:** about 4 dozen.

WALNUT TASSIES

Deanne Ford, Jerome, Idaho

(PICTURED ON PAGE 56)

Dainty and delicious, these nut-filled tarts are an old-fashioned favorite in our family. They make a pretty gift when packaged in a decorated egg carton with colored paper liners in each cup.

     1 cup butter, softened
     2 packages (3 ounces *each*) cream cheese, softened
     2 cups all-purpose flour
FILLING:
     1 tablespoon butter, melted
     1 egg, beaten
   3/4 cup packed brown sugar
Pinch salt
     1 teaspoon vanilla extract
   2/3 cup chopped walnuts
Halved candied cherries, optional

In a mixing bowl, blend butter, cream cheese and flour. Chill. Divide dough into fourths; divide each fourth into 12 small balls. Press each ball into miniature tart or muffin pans. For filling, combine all ingredients except cherries; fill tarts 3/4 full. Place on baking sheets. Bake at 325° for 25-30 minutes or until crust is browned and filling set. Cool in pans on wire rack for 10 minutes. Remove from pans. If desired, garnish with candied cherries. **Yield:** 4 dozen.

TEATIME. Opposite page, clockwise from top: Chocolate Snowballs, Walnut Tassies, Raspberry Bars, Cottage Cheese Cookies (recipes on this page), Date Bars (p. 58).

RASPBERRY BARS

Abby Kuhn, Ellsworth, Maine

(PICTURED ON PAGE 56)

This is a favorite finger food for Valentine's Day parties because it looks so festive. Here in snowy Maine, these bars are also fun to make on a "snow day" when our normal routine shifts to a vacation day.

   1/3 cup sugar
1-1/2 cups all-purpose flour
   3/4 cup butter *or* margarine
     2 eggs, *separated*
     1 cup raspberry jam
     1 cup broken walnuts
   1/2 cup sugar

In a bowl, combine sugar, flour, butter and egg yolks. Press into a greased 13-in. x 9-in. x 2-in. baking pan. Bake at 350° for 15 minutes or until golden. Cool. Spread jam over crust; sprinkle with nuts. In a mixing bowl, beat egg whites and sugar until stiff; spread meringue over nuts. Bake for another 25 minutes. To cut, use a knife dipped in hot water. **Yield:** 3-4 dozen.

"Every day I think of my mother, who was Grandmother to my children, for there are so many things around me to remind me of her. But most of all, when I make one of her dessert recipes and take a bite, I am transported back to a time long ago when life seemed easy and no dark clouds hovered."

—Sue Svrcek, Donora, Pennsylvania

COTTAGE CHEESE COOKIES

Linda Hobbs, Albion, New York

(PICTURED ON PAGE 56)

These delicate, puffy turnover cookies are sparked with raspberry and almond—delightful with afternoon tea.

     2 cups sifted all-purpose flour
     1 cup butter (no substitutes)
     1 cup plus 2 tablespoons creamed-style small-curd cottage cheese
Raspberry jam
GLAZE:
     1 cup confectioners' sugar
   1/8 teaspoon almond extract
Milk

Place flour in a medium mixing bowl; cut in butter as for pie crust. Blend in cottage cheese until mixture forms a ball (can use a food processor). Chill 1 hour. On a floured board, roll dough to 1/8-in. thickness. Cut with a 3-in. round cutter. Place a level 1/4 teaspoon of jam in center of each cookie. Moisten edges and fold in half; seal tightly with a fork. Place on lightly greased baking sheets; prick tops with fork. Bake at 400° for 15 minutes or until lightly browned. Cool on a wire rack. For glaze, mix sugar, extract and enough milk to make thin spreading consistency; drizzle on cooled cookies. **Yield:** 4 dozen.

DATE BARS

Dorothy DeLeske, Scottsdale, Arizona

(PICTURED ON PAGE 56)

I used to be the cafeteria manager at a grade school and these bars were always a hit.

2-1/2 cups chopped dates
1/4 cup sugar
1-1/2 cups water
1/3 cup broken walnuts, optional
1-1/4 cups sifted all-purpose flour
1 teaspoon salt
1/2 teaspoon baking soda
1-1/2 cups quick-cooking oats
1 cup packed brown sugar
1/2 cup butter
1 tablespoon water

In a saucepan, combine dates, sugar and water. Cook, stirring frequently, until thick. Stir in nuts if desired. Meanwhile, in a mixing bowl, sift together flour, salt and baking soda. Add oats and brown sugar. Cut in butter until crumbly. Add water and mix lightly. Press half into a greased 13-in. x 9-in. x 2-in. baking pan. Spread date mixture on top. Cover with remaining oat mixture; pat lightly. Bake at 350° for 35-40 minutes or until lightly browned. **Yield:** 3-4 dozen.

GROSSMUTTER'S PEPPERNUTS

Marilyn Kutzli, Clinton, Iowa

Before Christmas, my grandmother would bake peppernuts and store them until the "big day". When the house would smell like anise, we knew the holiday season had arrived.

3 eggs
2 cups sugar
2-3/4 cups all-purpose flour
1 teaspoon anise extract *or* crushed anise seed

In a large mixing bowl, beat eggs and sugar at medium speed for 15 minutes. Reduce speed and slowly add flour and anise. Mix until well combined. On a lightly floured board, shape dough into ropes about 1/2 in. in diameter. Chill 1 hour. Slice ropes into 1/2-in. lengths. Place on greased cookie sheets. Bake at 350° for 6-8 minutes or until set. Cookies will harden upon standing. When cool, store in airtight containers; they are best if allowed to age before serving. **Yield:** 30 dozen.

BAKI'S OLD-WORLD COOKIES

Marilyn Louise Riggenbach, Ravenna, Ohio

My uncles have always called these "cupcake cookies" because of the unique and pretty way they're baked. My maternal grandmother mixed up many a batch.

1 cup sugar
1 cup butter, softened
2 eggs
1 cup ground walnuts
1-1/2 cups all-purpose flour

1 teaspoon ground cloves
1/2 teaspoon ground cinnamon
2 teaspoons vanilla extract
Shortening
Confectioners' sugar

In a mixing bowl, cream sugar and butter. Add eggs, one at a time, beating well after each addition, and nuts. Sift together flour and spices; add with vanilla to creamed mixture. Chill 1 hour. Using shortening, liberally grease muffin tins or individual 3-in. tins or tart shells. Fill tins 1/3 to 1/2 full and press dough around sides, leaving depression in center. (If dough is too soft as you press into tins, add more flour.) Bake at 350° for about 18 minutes or until light brown. Cool 2 minutes; tap tins to remove cookies. Dust with confectioners' sugar. **Yield:** 2-3 dozen.

GINGER-CREAM BARS

Carol Nagelkirk, Holland, Michigan

I rediscovered this old-time recipe recently and found it's everyone's favorite. Even 4-year-olds have asked for these frosted bars as nursery school treats.

1 cup sugar
1 cup butter, softened
2 cups all-purpose flour
1 teaspoon salt
2 teaspoons baking soda
1 tablespoon ground cinnamon
1 tablespoon ground cloves
1 tablespoon ground ginger
2 eggs
1/2 cup molasses
1 cup hot coffee
FROSTING:
1/2 cup butter, softened
1 package (3 ounces) cream cheese, softened
2 cups confectioners' sugar
2 teaspoons vanilla extract
Chopped nuts, optional

In a medium bowl, cream sugar and butter. Sift together flour, salt, soda and spices; add to creamed mixture. Add eggs, one at a time, beating well after each addition, and molasses. Blend in coffee. Spread in a 15-in. x 10-in. x 1-in. baking pan. Bake at 350° for 20-25 minutes. Cool. For frosting, cream butter and cream cheese; add sugar and vanilla. Spread over bars. Top with nuts if desired. **Yield:** 5-6 dozen.

STRAWBERRY CREAM COOKIES

Glenna Aberle, Sabetha, Kansas

This cream cheese cookie looks lovely on a tea tray.

1 cup butter, softened
1 cup sugar
1 package (3 ounces) cream cheese, softened
1 tablespoon vanilla extract
1 egg yolk, room temperature
2-1/2 cups all-purpose flour
Strawberry jam, room temperature

In a mixing bowl, cream butter, sugar and cream cheese.

Add vanilla and egg yolk; mix well. Add flour and blend. Chill. Shape dough into 1-in. balls and place on ungreased cookie sheets. Using a floured thimble, press a hole in center of each cookie; fill with 1/4 teaspoon jam. Bake at 350° for 10-12 minutes. **Yield:** 5 dozen.

APPLE-CHIP COOKIES
Mrs. Dean Zahs, Ainsworth, Iowa

These scrumptious apple cookies never last for long in our cookie jar.

        1/4 cup butter *or* margarine, softened
          1 cup packed brown sugar
        1/2 cup cream
          1 egg
          2 cups all-purpose flour
        1/2 teaspoon baking soda
        1/2 teaspoon salt
        1/4 teaspoon ground nutmeg
          1 cup chopped pared apples
        1/2 cup chocolate *or* butterscotch chips
          1 cup chopped nuts
GLAZE:
          3 tablespoons butter *or* margarine, melted
          1 teaspoon ground cinnamon
          2 tablespoons cream
          2 cups confectioners' sugar

In a mixing bowl, cream butter and sugar. Beat in cream and egg. Combine dry ingredients; add to creamed mixture. Fold in apples, chips and nuts. Drop by teaspoonfuls onto greased cookie sheets. Bake at 350° for 12-15 minutes. Do not overbake. For glaze, combine all ingredients; spread over cooled cookies. **Yield:** about 3 dozen.

SWEDISH ALMOND RUSKS
Judy Videen, Moorhead, Minnesota

Not too sweet, these nutty, crunchy cookies go well with a cup of hot coffee…and travel well in care packages, too!

          1 cup butter, softened
    1-3/4 cups sugar
          2 eggs
          2 teaspoons almond extract
          5 cups all-purpose flour
          1 teaspoon ground cardamom
          1 teaspoon baking soda
          1 cup (8 ounces) sour cream
          1 cup finely chopped almonds

In a mixing bowl, cream butter and sugar. Add eggs, one at a time, beating well after each addition. Stir in extract. Sift together flour, cardamom and soda; add alternately with sour cream to creamed mixture. Fold in almonds. Divide dough into six parts; shape into rolls (like refrigerated cookie dough). Place three each on two greased cookie sheets. Bake at 350° for about 30 minutes or until light brown. Remove rolls to cutting board. Using a sharp knife, slice rolls diagonally 1/2 in. thick. Place cookies on sheets; return to oven and bake until light brown. Cool; store in tightly covered containers. **Yield:** 6 dozen.

FRUIT 'N' NUT BARS
Mrs. John Nagel, Deerbrook, Wisconsin

Here's a healthy treat that grandchildren are sure to enjoy. For convenient snacking, wrap the bars individually in plastic wrap.

    1-1/4 cups chopped almonds
          1 jar (2 ounces) sesame seeds
          4 cups quick-cooking oats
          1 cup dark seedless raisins
          1 cup light corn syrup
        2/3 cup vegetable oil
        1/2 cup hulled sunflower seeds
        1/2 cup toasted wheat germ
        1/2 cup nonfat dry milk powder
          2 teaspoons ground cinnamon
          1 teaspoon vanilla extract
        1/2 teaspoon salt

In a large bowl, combine all ingredients; mix well. Press mixture firmly and evenly into a greased 15-in. x 10-in. x 1-in. baking pan. Bake at 350° for 25 minutes or until golden brown. Cool in pan on wire rack at least 2 hours. Store in refrigerator. **Yield:** 18 bars.

LEMON SNOWDROPS
Bernice Martinoni, Petaluma, California
(PICTURED ON OUR COVER)

This crunchy butter cookie has a perfect lemon filling. I usually save them for special, festive occasions.

          1 cup butter, softened
        1/2 cup confectioners' sugar
          1 teaspoon lemon extract
          2 cups all-purpose flour
        1/4 teaspoon salt
LEMON BUTTER FILLING:
          1 egg, lightly beaten
        2/3 cup sugar
          3 tablespoons lemon juice
Grated peel of 1 lemon
1-1/2 tablespoons butter, softened
Additional confectioners' sugar

In a mixing bowl, cream butter and sugar; add extract. Sift together flour and salt; add to creamed mixture and mix well. Roll level teaspoonfuls into balls; flatten slightly. Place 1 in. apart on ungreased cookie sheets. Bake at 350° for 8-10 minutes. Meanwhile, for filling, combine egg, sugar, lemon juice, peel and butter in the top of a double boiler. Cook over hot water until thick, stirring constantly. Cool. Spread filling on half the cookies and top each with another cookie; roll in confectioners' sugar. **Yield:** 2-1/2-3 dozen.

Ice Cream Desserts

ON summer days when the sun was hot enough to burn a bare foot, Grandma could cool off the crowd lickety-split with a homemade ice cream dessert. Those frozen confections were delicious enough to enjoy even when a cold wind was blowing!

Grandma combined sugar, egg yolks and farm-fresh cream with fruit or chopped nuts and other natural ingredients. Sometimes she chilled the mixture in a crumb crust.

More often, she poured the concoction into a crank freezer packed with ice and salt and let family members help turn the handle while the ice cream hardened. After waiting what seemed an eternity, eating that smooth, sweet treat was pure heaven!

Next time you're looking for a melt-in-your-mouth dessert—literally—do your family and friends a "flavor" and try one of the irresistible ice cream desserts in this chapter!

CHOCOLATE ICE CREAM
Kathryn Herman, Villisca, Iowa
(PICTURED ON PAGE 60)

This is, without a doubt, the best ice cream I've ever had. Our family loves to make homemade ice cream when we get together for birthday dinners, and this is our favorite flavor.

- 1 quart whole milk
- 1 egg, beaten
- 2 egg yolks, beaten
- 2 cups sugar
- 1/3 cup unsweetened cocoa
- 2 tablespoons all-purpose flour
- 2 cans (12 ounces *each*) evaporated milk
- 2 tablespoons vanilla extract

Milk

In a heavy saucepan, combine first six ingredients. Cook until thickened. Add evaporated milk; bring to a boil. Remove from heat and cool. Add vanilla. Pour into the cylinder of an ice cream freezer; add enough milk to fill cylinder 3/4 full. Freeze according to manufacturer's directions. **Yield:** about 2-1/2 quarts.

PARLOR PASSIONS. Opposite page, top to bottom: Butter Pecan Ice Cream (p. 62), Chocolate Ice Cream (above) with Fudge Sundae Sauce (p. 62), Banana Split Dessert (right).

CARAMEL ICE CREAM
Bonnie Partin, Nehawka, Nebraska

Every Fourth of July, our family would gather for a picnic, fireworks and scoops of my mother's special ice cream. I can also remember sitting around the coal stove eating it at my sister's house. Boy, was it good!

- 3 cups sugar, *divided*
- 4 eggs, beaten
- 4 tablespoons all-purpose flour
- 4 cups milk
- 1 teaspoon vanilla extract

Whipping cream

In a heavy skillet, brown 2 cups sugar, stirring constantly, until caramelized, being careful not to scorch it. Immediately combine eggs, remaining sugar, flour and milk in a large saucepan. Smooth out any lumps and bring to a boil. Carefully add caramelized sugar and stir constantly until mixture is melted. Remove from the heat; add vanilla. Pour into the cylinder of an ice cream freezer; add enough whipping cream to fill cylinder 3/4 full. Freeze according to manufacturer's directions. **Yield:** about 1 gallon.

BANANA SPLIT DESSERT
Mrs. Elmer Thorsheim, Radcliffe, Iowa
(PICTURED ON PAGE 60)

Here's a mouth-watering make-ahead dessert that looks scrumptious...and tastes as good as it looks!

- 3-1/2 cups graham cracker crumbs
- 2/3 cup butter, melted
- 4 to 5 bananas
- 1/2 gallon Neapolitan ice cream (block carton)
- 1 cup chopped walnuts
- 1 cup (6 ounces) chocolate chips
- 1/2 cup butter
- 2 cups confectioners' sugar
- 1 can (12 ounces) evaporated milk
- 1 teaspoon vanilla extract
- 1 pint whipping cream

Combine crumbs and melted butter. Reserve 1/2 cup; press remaining crumbs into the bottom of a 15-in. x 11-in. x 2-in. baking pan or 15-in. x 10-in. x 2-in. baking dish. Slice bananas crosswise and layer over crust. Cut ice cream crosswise into eighths; place over bananas. Spread edges of ice cream slices to cover bananas and form a smooth layer. Sprinkle with nuts. Freeze until firm. In a saucepan, melt chocolate chips and butter; add sugar and milk. Cook, stirring constantly, over medium heat until slightly thickened and smooth. Remove from the heat; add vanilla. Cool. Pour over ice cream; freeze until firm. Whip cream until stiff; spread over chocolate layer; top with reserved crumbs. Store in freezer (will keep for several weeks). Remove from freezer about 10 minutes before serving. **Yield:** 25 servings.

FUDGE SUNDAE SAUCE
Tammy Mackie, Seward, Nebraska
(PICTURED ON PAGE 60)

My father-in-law introduced this recipe to the family. It has a nice flavor and is a special favorite of our four children's.

- **2 cups (12 ounces) semisweet chocolate chips**
- **2 squares (1 ounce *each*) unsweetened chocolate**
- **1 cup whipping cream**
- **1/4 cup cold coffee**
- **Dash salt**
- **1 teaspoon vanilla extract**

In a medium saucepan, combine chocolate, cream, coffee and salt. Heat on low, stirring constantly, until chocolate is melted. Remove from the heat; stir in vanilla. Cover and refrigerate. Reheat to serve over your favorite ice cream. **Yield:** 2-1/2 cups.

BUTTER PECAN ICE CREAM
Connie Webb, Needham, Indiana
(PICTURED ON PAGE 60)

Making homemade ice cream has long been our family's favorite pastime, and this butter pecan recipe is our first choice in fall.

- **2 eggs, lightly beaten**
- **1/2 cup packed light brown sugar**
- **1 cup sugar**
- **2 cups half-and-half cream**
- **1/4 teaspoon salt**
- **2 cups milk, scalded and cooled**
- **1-1/2 teaspoons vanilla extract**
- **2 tablespoons butter**
- **1 cup finely chopped pecans**

In a heavy saucepan or top of a double boiler, combine eggs, sugars, cream and salt. Cook over low heat, stirring constantly, until mixture coats a spoon. Cool. Add milk and vanilla. Refrigerate for several hours. In a skillet, melt butter. Add pecans and saute on medium heat, stirring constantly, being careful not to burn them. Cool. Pour egg mixture into the cylinder of an ice cream freezer; add pecans, stirring slightly to distribute. Freeze according to manufacturer's directions. When frozen, pack ice cream in airtight containers and store in freezer. **Yield:** 2 quarts.

CHOCOLATE MALT SHOPPE PIE
Beth Wanek, Little Chute, Wisconsin

I especially like serving this dessert at a cookout or at any event where there are children—it's always a big hit!

- **1-1/2 cups chocolate cookie crumbs**
- **1/4 cup butter *or* margarine, melted**
- **1 pint vanilla ice cream, softened**
- **1/2 cup crushed malted milk balls**
- **2 tablespoons milk, *divided***
- **3 tablespoons instant chocolate malted milk powder**

- **3 tablespoons marshmallow creme**
- **1 cup whipping cream**
- **Additional whipped cream**
- **Additional malted milk balls**

Combine crumbs and butter; press into a 9-in. pie pan. Freeze. Meanwhile, blend ice cream, crushed malted milk balls and 1 tablespoon milk in a mixing bowl. Spoon into crust; freeze for 1 hour. In a mixing bowl, blend malted milk powder, marshmallow creme and remaining milk. Stir in whipping cream; whip until soft peaks form. Spread over ice cream layer. Freeze several hours or overnight. Before serving, dollop whipped cream around edges of pie and place a malted milk ball on top of each dollop. **Yield:** 6-8 servings.

SUPER STRAWBERRY SHERBET
Anne Dickens, Sarasota, Florida
(PICTURED ON PAGE 63)

This cool, smooth summertime treat is nice to have ready in the freezer for a special dessert.

- **4 quarts fresh strawberries, sliced**
- **4 cups sugar**
- **2-2/3 cups milk**
- **2/3 cup orange juice**
- **1/8 teaspoon ground cinnamon**

Combine strawberries and sugar; let stand until juicy, about 1-1/2 hours. Mash or puree in a blender in several batches. Add milk, orange juice and cinnamon; blend well. Pour into the cylinder of an ice cream freezer and freeze according to manufacturer's directions, or pour into ice cube trays without dividers. If preparing in trays, freeze about 3 hours, stirring two or three times. **Yield:** about 1 gallon.

GRANDMA'S ORANGE MILK SHERBET
Marilynn Engelbrecht, Harrisonville, Missouri
(PICTURED ON PAGE 63)

My dear grandma made this sherbet for my birthday party in the 1930's. She squeezed whole oranges to get the juice for it. I often double the recipe...it's so refreshing on a hot summer day.

- **1-1/2 cups orange juice**
- **3/4 cup sugar**
- **3 cups milk, scalded and cooled**
- **1 can (16 ounces) crushed pineapple in natural juices**

In a bowl, combine orange juice and sugar; blend thoroughly. Add milk and mix. Place in chilled ice cube trays without dividers or a shallow pan; freeze until mushy. Place mixture in a mixing bowl and whip. Add pineapple and juices. Return to trays or pan and freeze. **Yield:** about 2 quarts.

DISH IT OUT. Opposite page, from left to right: Grandma's Orange Milk Sherbet, Super Strawberry Sherbet (above), Lemon/Orange Ice (p. 64).

LEMON/ORANGE ICE
Karen Zwieg, Lowry, Minnesota
(PICTURED ON PAGE 63)

This recipe originated years ago with my grandmother. It's her favorite ice cream, and I always think of her when I make it. She still likes serving it to all her many grandchildren!

Juice of 6 lemons
Juice of 7 oranges
3-1/2 cups sugar
  1 pint whipping cream
  1 quart whole milk

In a large bowl, combine juices, sugar, cream and milk. Mix well. Pour into the cylinder of an ice cream freezer and freeze according to manufacturer's directions. Serve immediately for a soft consistency or place in refrigerator/freezer. **Yield:** 2 quarts.

CARAMEL PECAN ICE CREAM DESSERT
Mary Wright, Morriston, Ontario

My mother passed this old-time recipe on to me because she knew I'd want to make it...I love desserts, especially this one!

1-3/4 cups all-purpose flour
  1 cup chopped pecans
  1 cup packed brown sugar
  1 cup quick-cooking oats
  1 cup butter, melted
1-1/2 cups caramel ice cream topping
  2 quarts vanilla ice cream, softened

In a large bowl, combine flour, pecans, sugar and oats. Add butter; mix well. Spread in a thin layer on a large baking sheet with sides. Bake at 400° for 15 minutes, stirring occasionally, or until golden. Crumble while warm; cool. Press half of crumb mixture into a 13-in. x 9-in. x 2-in. baking pan. Drizzle with half of caramel sauce; spread with ice cream. Top with remaining caramel sauce and crumbs. Cover and freeze. Remove from freezer 10 minutes before serving. **Yield:** 12-15 servings.

BING CHERRY ICE CREAM SAUCE
Jane Thibeault, Oxford, Massachusetts
(PICTURED ON PAGE 65)

Pour this over your favorite ice cream for a sweet-tart treat!

  1 can (16 ounces) pitted dark sweet cherries
  2 tablespoons cornstarch
1/4 teaspoon almond extract
Ice cream *or* frozen vanilla custard

Drain cherries, reserving juice. Place juice and cornstarch in a saucepan. Cook, stirring constantly, until thickened. Stir in extract and cherries. Serve warm over ice cream or Old-Fashioned Frozen Vanilla Custard (see page 66). **Yield:** 4-6 servings.

CHILLING DISCOVERY. Did you know that frozen desserts first became delicacies when the Romans of Julius Caesar's day fetched mountain snow and flavored it with fruit juices?

Centuries later, recipes for "Cream Ice" were introduced in Europe and eventually spread to America. Dolly Madison is said to have reversed the name, adding "Ice Cream" to the White House menu. It's been a dairy delight ever since!

STRAWBERRY ICE CREAM
Esther Johnson, Merrill, Wisconsin

What could be better than a tubful of luscious, homemade ice cream made with fresh strawberries? Having an ice cream social at church with more of the same!

  6 egg yolks
  2 cups milk
  1 cup sugar
1/4 teaspoon salt
  1 teaspoon vanilla extract
  2 cups whipping cream
  2 cups crushed fresh strawberries, sweetened

Place egg yolks and milk in the top of a double boiler; beat. Add sugar and salt. Cook over simmering water, stirring until mixture is thickened and coats a metal spoon. Cool. Add vanilla, cream and strawberries. Pour into the cylinder of an ice cream freezer and freeze according to manufacturer's directions. **Yield:** about 1-1/2 quarts.

ICE CREAM SUPREME
Kathleen Clapp, Blue Hill, Maine

Summers here in Maine are too short to spend a lot of time in the kitchen, so we're always looking for simple, quick recipes to make. This fast dessert fits our family of ice cream lovers fine!

  1 cup (6 ounces) chocolate chips
1/3 cup creamy peanut butter
  3 cups crispy rice cereal
1/2 gallon vanilla ice cream, softened

In a saucepan, melt chocolate and peanut butter together. Add cereal; mix until coated. Spread on waxed paper to cool. Reserve 3/4 cup; combine remaining mixture with ice cream. Spread in a springform pan; top with remaining cereal mixture. Freeze 4 hours or overnight. Recipe can be doubled. **Yield:** 10 servings.

CREAMY CONFECTIONS. On the opposite page: Frozen Grasshopper Torte, Old-Fashioned Frozen Vanilla Custard (p. 66) with Bing Cherry Ice Cream Sauce (left).

FROZEN GRASSHOPPER TORTE

Elma Penner, Oak Bluff, Manitoba

(PICTURED ON PAGE 65)

I first made this tasty torte for a ladies' meeting at our church, and it went over very well. I've made it often since then and have received many compliments from young and old alike.

> 4 cups crushed cream-filled chocolate cookies
>   (about 40)
> 1/4 cup butter, melted
> 1 pint vanilla ice cream, slightly softened
> 1/4 cup milk
> 1 jar (7 ounces) marshmallow creme
> 1/4 to 1/2 teaspoon peppermint extract
> Few drops green food coloring
> 2 cups heavy cream, whipped

Combine cookie crumbs and butter. Reserve 1/4 cup; press remaining crumbs into the bottom of a 9-in. springform pan, two 9-in. pie plates or a 13-in. x 9-in. x 2-in. baking dish. Chill for 30 minutes. Spread ice cream over crust. Freeze. Meanwhile, in a bowl, combine milk and marshmallow creme; stir until well blended. Add extract and food coloring. Fold in whipped cream. Spoon over ice cream and sprinkle with reserved crumbs. Freeze until firm. **Yield:** 12-16 servings.

Ice Cream Sunday

When I was young, making homemade hand-cranked ice cream on Sundays was a special summertime "chore" for the whole family.

While Mom or Grandma mixed the ice cream and filled the canister, my brother or a cousin and I would toss a few rag rugs in a wagon and race to the icehouse about 6 blocks away. We'd load up enough ice to chill the ice cream, as well as to keep several pitchers of iced tea and lemonade cold. Before covering the ice with the rags, the "ice man" always chipped off a bit for us to eat on the way home.

We took turns pushing and pulling the wagon, hurrying to keep the ice from melting under the blazing sun. The last block was the toughest—it was all uphill!

When at last we reached home, all the men and older kids took turns cranking the handle. Dad always added the salt and ice. He was generous with the salt, though, so when that lid came off, the ice cream on top was a bit salty (but the best there was, Dad and I thought!). In fact, Dad and I liked to eat our ice cream with saltine crackers, even though Mom always baked a big coconut cake to go with it.

We have an electric ice cream maker now, which makes ice cream for our five children to enjoy. And I still eat mine with saltines. But it sure doesn't taste like it did when we worked harder for it!

—*Sylvan Ashbache, Lansing, Iowa*

VERY CHERRY ICE CREAM

Sandy Hold, Sapulpa, Oklahoma

This recipe is a favorite at family get-togethers...everyone, from my 80-year-old grandmother to my 2-year-old daughter, enjoys it. I usually mix and chill the ingredients early in the day, then later everyone gets in on cranking the ice cream!

> 1 pound fresh *or* frozen pitted dark sweet
>   cherries, coarsely chopped (about 1-3/4 cups)
> 1/2 cup sugar
> 1 package (3 ounces) cherry-flavored gelatin
> 1 cup boiling water
> 1 package (3 ounces) cook and serve vanilla
>   pudding mix
> 3-1/2 cups milk
> 2 cups heavy cream
> 2 teaspoons vanilla extract

In a large bowl, combine cherries and sugar; set aside. Dissolve gelatin in boiling water; set aside. Cook pudding according to package directions, using 3-1/2 cups milk. Add to cherries. Stir in cream, vanilla and prepared gelatin. Refrigerate, stirring occasionally, until cold. Pour into the cylinder of an ice cream freezer and freeze according to manufacturer's directions. **Yield:** 2 quarts.

OLD-FASHIONED FROZEN VANILLA CUSTARD

Mrs. Duaine Kurtzbein, Montevideo, Minnesota

(PICTURED ON PAGE 65)

Not too long ago, I found this recipe for a frozen treat we used to eat when we went to Grandma's house. Now, whenever I make it, it reminds me of her. She loved to bake, and so do I.

> 1 cup half-and-half cream
> 2/3 cup sugar
> 3 eggs, beaten
> 1 cup whipping cream
> 1 teaspoon vanilla extract
> 1/4 teaspoon salt

In a heavy saucepan, combine first three ingredients. Cook, stirring constantly, until thickened. Cool. Pour into chilled ice cube trays without dividers or a shallow pan. Freeze to a mush (do not freeze hard). Whip cream; add vanilla and salt. Fold into partially frozen mixture. Return to trays or pan and freeze. **Yield:** 1 quart.

FROM GRANDMA'S KITCHEN:
Old-Fashioned Ice Cream Roll

Darlene Markel

"I serve my grandmother's Old-Fashioned Ice Cream Roll only on special occasions, because my grandmother was a very special lady."

One of Darlene Markel's most treasured items is a *big* family cookbook. It contains 861 recipes from 363 relatives in 21 states, five Canadian provinces and even Germany! Her favorite of them all? It's a dessert her grandmother served on holidays and other special occasions.

"When I think of my grandmother, I think of her wonderful Old-Fashioned Ice Cream Roll," says Darlene, who lives with her husband and two children in Roseburg, Oregon. "It was always a special treat for us grandkids."

Darlene remembers how all the relatives would gather together for dessert and coffee at her grandparents' home in Mandan, North Dakota. Her grandmother would lengthen the large parlor table with extra leaves and cover it with an assortment of homemade desserts.

"We'd always have angel food cake with white icing, various German cookies, perfect little rosettes that Grandpa made, and my favorite, Grandma's Ice Cream Roll," Darlene recalls. "Grandma would serve it with warm caramel sauce, which would melt the ice cream slightly. Oooh...it was *so* good!"

Darlene had to act fast to get a slice of that delicious roll, however, since she was among 38 grandchildren, more than 30 great-grandchildren and 22

aunts and uncles! "Relatives would be squeezed around the table, standing along the sides and at the kitchen counter—wherever they could find room to eat!" she says with a chuckle.

Darlene's grandmother learned to bake for a crowd by having a large family—a husband and 11 children. Yet she never tired of catering to their individual tastes, Darlene points out. "My dad remembers how Grandma spoiled her kids with German dishes and baked goodies even when times were rough. She'd often make food two or three different ways—meat would be served with gravy or tomato sauce, for instance—just to please everyone's palate!

"She did the same for her grandchildren...she was one of those grandmothers every person hopes to have," says Darlene, who now possesses the cherished apron her grandmother always wore in the kitchen. She also seems to have acquired her grandmother's knack for baking.

In the midst of renovating a 1905 farmhouse with her family, Darlene enjoys treating them to a different pie or dessert nearly every day. But the dessert she plans to serve once renovations are complete is —you guessed it—her grandmother's Old-Fashioned Ice Cream Roll.

OLD-FASHIONED ICE CREAM ROLL

3/4 teaspoon baking powder
1/4 teaspoon salt
  4 eggs
3/4 cup sugar
3/4 cup all-purpose flour
  1 teaspoon vanilla extract
1/2 gallon vanilla ice cream, slightly softened
CARAMEL SAUCE:
  1 cup packed brown sugar
1/2 cup sugar
1/4 teaspoon salt
1/2 cup light corn syrup
  1 cup whipping cream
Chopped pecans, optional

In a large mixing bowl, combine baking powder, salt and eggs; beat until golden yellow. Add sugar gradually until mixture becomes thick and light-colored. Add flour a little at a time. Stir in vanilla. Spread into a greased and waxed paper-lined 15-in. x 10-in. x 1-in. baking pan. Bake at 375° for 10-12 minutes or until light gold. Turn out onto a dish towel sprinkled with confectioners' sugar. Peel off waxed paper and roll up, jelly-roll style; cool. When cool, unroll and spread with ice cream. Roll up again; freeze until firm. For sauce, combine sugars, salt and corn syrup in a saucepan. Cook until mixture comes to a full boil. Remove from heat; cool slightly. Add cream and stir well. To serve, slice frozen ice cream roll and pour warm sauce over. Top with pecans if desired. **Yield:** 8-10 servings (sauce makes 2 cups). **Variation:** Use strawberry ice cream instead of vanilla and eliminate caramel sauce. Garnish with fresh strawberries and whipped cream.

Puddings & Pies

"Pass me a piece of the past, please!"

THE *BEST* puddings and pies are the tried-and-true, the ones lovingly prepared in the cozy kitchens of grandmothers and great-grandmothers.

Even in lean times, Grandma always managed to whip up warm and wonderful desserts that made everyone feel like kings—richly crusted pastries bubbling over with luscious fruit fillings...creamy custards and perfect puddings made with fresh milk from the farm. A slice of fruit pie was the prize of the harvest season, and a bowl of chocolate pudding could instantly bring a smile.

With the following recipes, you and your family can enjoy these familiar, old-fashioned favorites all over again. See? Reliving a bit of the past *is* "easy as pie"!

OLD-FASHIONED CHOCOLATE PUDDING
Amber Sampson, Somonauk, Illinois
(PICTURED ON PAGE 68)

One of the nice things about this easy pudding is you don't have to stand and stir it. It's a must for us year-round! I also make it into a pie with a graham cracker crust that our grandchildren love.

2 cups milk
2 tablespoons butter *or* margarine
2 squares (1 ounce *each*) unsweetened chocolate
2/3 cup sugar
1/3 cup all-purpose flour
1/4 teaspoon salt
2 egg yolks, beaten
1/2 teaspoon vanilla extract
Whipped cream, optional

In the top of a double boiler, heat milk, butter and chocolate until the chocolate melts. Chocolate may appear curdled. Combine sugar, flour and salt. Sprinkle over chocolate mixture. *Do not stir.* Cover the mixture and cook on medium-low for 20 minutes. Beat mixture until smooth. Quickly add egg yolks; beat well. Cook 2 additional minutes. Remove from the heat and stir in vanilla. Pour into dessert glasses; chill. Serve with whipped cream if desired. **Yield:** 4 servings.

TEMPTING TRIO. Opposite page, from top to bottom: Grandma's Sour Cream Raisin Pie (p. 77), Cherry Berry Pie (p. 77), Old-Fashioned Chocolate Pudding (above).

LEMON SNOW PUDDING
Eula Voehl, Ottumwa, Iowa

My mother first served this light and refreshing dessert at a dinner for my brother, his new bride and their wedding guests back in the early '40's. When I got married in '47, I made sure I had the recipe.

1-1/2 cups water
Juice of 1 large lemon (1/4 cup)
3/4 cup sugar
1/2 teaspoon salt
2 tablespoons cornstarch
2 tablespoons cold water
3 egg whites
CUSTARD SAUCE:
3 egg yolks
1/8 teaspoon salt
1/2 cup sugar
1 cup milk, scalded and slightly cooled
1 teaspoon vanilla extract

In a medium saucepan, combine water, lemon juice, sugar and salt. Heat to boiling. Make a thin paste from cornstarch and cold water; add to saucepan. Cook and stir over low heat until smooth and clear. In a small mixing bowl, beat egg whites until stiff peaks form. Add to saucepan and beat with a wire whisk until mixed, about 2 minutes. Let stand 4 minutes. Remove from heat and cool. Meanwhile, for sauce, combine egg yolks, salt and sugar in a heavy saucepan. Gradually stir in milk. Cook over low heat, stirring constantly, until mixture coats a spoon. Remove from heat; immediately place pan in cold water to cool. Stir for 1-2 minutes. Add vanilla. Chill. To serve, spoon pudding into individual serving dishes and top with sauce. Sauce will settle to bottom of dish. Refrigerate leftovers. **Yield:** 6 servings.

BAKED CUSTARD
Deb Brass, Cedar Falls, Iowa

I first made this family recipe as a teenager and still enjoy it as a winter warm-up. My dad says it's the best custard he's ever eaten!

4 eggs
2/3 cup sugar
1/2 teaspoon salt
1/4 teaspoon ground nutmeg
1/4 teaspoon ground cinnamon
3 teaspoons vanilla extract
2-2/3 cups milk

In a mixing bowl, combine eggs, sugar, spices and vanilla. Blend in milk. Pour into a 1-1/2-qt. baking dish. Place baking dish in a cake pan in oven; add 1 in. water to pan. Bake at 325° for 1 hour or until a knife inserted near middle comes out clean. **Yield:** 6 servings.

RAISIN SURPRISE PUDDING
Myrna Sippel, Thompson, Illinois

A helping of this old-fashioned dessert reveals a sweet raisin sauce hidden inside.

        1 cup all-purpose flour
        1 cup sugar
        2 teaspoons baking powder
    1/2 cup milk
Pinch salt
        1 cup raisins
        1 cup packed brown sugar
        2 cups boiling water
        2 tablespoons butter
    1/2 teaspoon vanilla extract
Whipped cream

In a small bowl, combine flour, sugar, baking powder, milk and salt; stir until well blended. Spread evenly in a lightly greased 9-in. square baking dish. In a saucepan, combine raisins, brown sugar, water and butter. Bring to a boil. Stir in vanilla. Pour gently over flour mixture. *Do not stir.* Bake at 350° for 30 minutes. Serve warm with whipped cream. **Yield:** 9 servings.

CAJUN BREAD PUDDING
Linda Walter, Jetmore, Kansas

This is my husband's favorite dessert, and it's a perfect dish for a crowd, too.

4-3/4 cups milk, *divided*
        4 eggs
    2/3 cup sugar
    1/4 teaspoon salt
        1 teaspoon vanilla extract
    1/3 cup butter, softened
      11 cups cubed French bread (1-inch cubes)
    1/2 teaspoon ground cinnamon
    2/3 cup raisins, optional
    2/3 cup chopped pecans, optional
PRALINE SAUCE:
    1/4 cup water
    1/3 cup packed brown sugar
    1/3 cup corn syrup
    1/2 cup coarsely chopped pecans
    1/2 teaspoon vanilla extract
        2 tablespoons butter
Dash salt

In a saucepan, heat 4 cups of milk until warm; set aside. In a large mixing bowl, combine remaining milk, eggs, sugar, salt and vanilla. Gradually add warmed milk, stirring constantly. Stir in butter. Add bread cubes; soak 10 minutes. Add cinnamon, and raisins and/or pecans if desired. Pour into a 13-in. x 9-in. x 2-in. baking pan. Bake at 400° for 45-60 minutes or until a knife inserted in center comes out clean. Meanwhile, for sauce, bring water to a boil in a saucepan. Add sugar; stir to dissolve. Add corn syrup. Bring to a boil; cook 15-20 seconds. Remove from the heat; add remaining ingredients. Cut pudding into squares and serve with sauce. **Yield:** 12 servings.

BREAD PUDDING
Donna Powell, Montgomery City, Missouri
(PICTURED ON PAGE 79)

I always make this recipe for my dad on his birthday and holidays. He says it tastes exactly like the bread pudding with nutmeg he enjoyed as a child.

        2 eggs
        2 cups scalded milk
        4 tablespoons butter *or* margarine
    3/4 cup sugar
    1/4 teaspoon salt
        1 teaspoon ground cinnamon
    1/2 teaspoon ground nutmeg
        1 teaspoon vanilla extract
4-1/2 to 5 cups soft bread cubes (about 9 slices)
    1/2 cup raisins, optional
VANILLA SAUCE:
    1/3 cup sugar
        2 tablespoons cornstarch
    1/4 teaspoon salt
1-2/3 cups water
        3 tablespoons butter *or* margarine
        2 teaspoons vanilla extract
    1/4 teaspoon ground nutmeg

In a large bowl, beat eggs lightly. Combine milk and butter; add to eggs along with sugar, spices and vanilla. Add bread cubes, and raisins if desired; stir gently. Pour into a well-greased 10-in. x 6-1/2-in. pan. Bake at 350° for 40-45 minutes or until a knife inserted 1 in. from edge comes out clean. Meanwhile, for sauce, combine sugar, cornstarch and salt in a saucepan. Stir in water; cook over medium heat for about 3 minutes. Remove from heat. Add butter, vanilla and nutmeg. Serve pudding and sauce warm. **Yield:** 6 servings.

OLD-FASHIONED RICE CUSTARD
Shirley Leister, West Chester, Pennsylvania

I don't remember where or how I found this dessert. When I took it to a family reunion many years ago, however, a great-uncle was sure I'd used my great-grandmother's recipe! I enjoy this custard warm or cold.

    1/2 cup uncooked long-grain rice
        4 cups milk, *divided*
    1/4 cup butter *or* margarine
        3 eggs
    3/4 cup sugar
        1 teaspoon vanilla extract
    1/4 teaspoon salt
    1/2 teaspoon ground nutmeg

In the top of a double boiler, combine rice and 2 cups milk. Cook, stirring occasionally, over boiling water until rice is tender and most of the water has evaporated, about 45 minutes. Stir in butter. In a mixing bowl, beat eggs. Blend in sugar, vanilla, salt and remaining milk; stir into hot rice mixture. Pour into a lightly greased 2-qt. casserole and top with nutmeg. Bake at 350° for 50 minutes or until firm. **Yield:** 6-8 servings.

BROWN SUGAR PUDDING CAKE
Violet Koecke, Bagley, Wisconsin

This is a wonderful old recipe that's been handed down through our family from my grandmother.

SAUCE:
- 1 cup packed brown sugar
- 1 tablespoon all-purpose flour
- 2 tablespoons butter, melted
- 1/4 teaspoon salt
- 2 cups boiling water

PUDDING:
- 2 tablespoons butter, melted
- 1/2 cup packed brown sugar
- 1 cup all-purpose flour
- 1 teaspoon baking powder
- 1/2 teaspoon salt
- 1/2 cup chopped nuts
- 1/2 cup milk

Combine all sauce ingredients. Pour into a 1-1/2-qt. baking dish; set aside. For pudding, beat butter and sugar in a mixing bowl. Combine flour, baking powder, salt and nuts; add alternately with milk to butter mixture. Spoon into baking dish. Bake at 350° for 40-45 minutes. **Yield:** 6-8 servings.

SAUCY MOCHA PUDDING
Kathy Koch, Smoky Lake, Alberta

Both my grandmother and mother made this dessert. Since I have five children (and four grandchildren now also), I've learned it's best to double the recipe! It's scrumptious with ice cream, whipped cream, or just plain!

SAUCE:
- 1/4 cup baking cocoa
- 1/2 cup sugar
- 1/2 cup packed brown sugar
- 1-1/2 cups hot strong coffee

CAKE:
- 1/3 cup butter *or* margarine
- 2/3 cup sugar
- 1 egg
- 1/2 teaspoon vanilla extract
- 1 cup all-purpose flour
- 1-1/2 teaspoons baking powder
- 1/4 teaspoon salt
- 1/3 cup milk

Ice cream *or* whipped cream, optional

In a saucepan, combine all sauce ingredients and keep warm. Meanwhile, in a large mixing bowl, beat butter, sugar, egg and vanilla until light and fluffy. Combine flour, baking powder and salt; add alternately with milk to the egg mixture. Spread into a greased 8-in. x 8-in. baking pan. Pour sauce over the batter. *Do not stir.* Bake at 350° for 45-50 minutes or until cake tests done. When finished, the cake will float in the hot mocha sauce. Serve warm with ice cream or whipped cream if desired. **Yield:** about 9 servings.

STEAMED CRANBERRY PUDDING
Bernadean Bichel, Woodbine, Georgia

One Christmas, my husband—a Navy chaplain for 20 years—had to spend the holidays overseas, away from our two children and me. At his request, I sent him this special recipe so he could have a taste of home.

PUDDING:
- 1/2 cup light molasses
- 1/2 cup hot water
- 2 teaspoons baking soda
- 1-1/2 cups all-purpose flour
- 2 cups fresh *or* frozen cranberries
- 1/2 teaspoon salt

SAUCE:
- 1 cup sugar
- 1 teaspoon cornstarch
- Dash salt
- 1 cup heavy cream
- 1/2 cup butter *or* margarine
- 1 teaspoon vanilla extract

In a mixing bowl, combine all pudding ingredients in order given. Pour into a well-greased 4-cup pudding mold. Place in a deep kettle on a rack. Fill kettle with boiling water to 1-in. depth; cover kettle and boil gently. Replace water as needed. Steam about 1 hour or until pudding tests done. Let stand 5 minutes before unmolding. Meanwhile, for sauce, combine sugar, cornstarch and salt in a saucepan. Add cream and butter. Cook and stir over medium heat until mixture begins to boil. Boil for about 1 minute. Remove from heat and stir in vanilla. Serve pudding and sauce warm. **Yield:** 6-8 servings.

APPLE HONEY TAPIOCA PUDDING
Amy Kraemer, Glencoe, Minnesota

I'm glad that apple season is long, since my family requests this pudding quite often!

- 4 cups sliced pared tart apples (cut in eighths)
- 3/4 cup honey
- 3 tablespoons butter
- 1/2 teaspoon salt
- 1 tablespoon lemon juice
- 1/2 teaspoon ground cinnamon
- 1/3 cup quick-cooking tapioca
- 2-1/2 cups water
- Cream, ice cream *or* whipped cream

In a medium saucepan, combine first six ingredients. Cover and simmer just until apples are tender. Using a slotted spoon, move apples into a bowl. Add tapioca and water to saucepan. Cook and stir until thickened and clear. Pour over apples. Serve warm with cream or ice cream, or cold with whipped cream. **Yield:** 6 servings.

> **MARVELOUS MERINGUE:** For a meringue topping that doesn't weep, never add more than 2 tablespoons of sugar for each egg white, spread the meringue all the way to the crust so it seals to the edge as it bakes, and make sure the oven is no hotter than 350°.

RASPBERRIES WITH SOUR CREAM CUSTARD

Elna Dobson, Sunnyvale, California

(PICTURED ON PAGE 75)

Every summer, my grandmother would treat us to her garden-fresh berries and this delicate, piquant soft custard sauce.

        1/2 cup sugar
        3 tablespoons cornstarch
        1/4 teaspoon salt
    1-1/4 cups milk
        4 eggs, beaten
        1/2 cup sour cream
    1-1/2 teaspoons vanilla extract
        2 pints fresh raspberries

In a medium saucepan, combine sugar, cornstarch and salt. Gradually stir in milk. Bring to a boil over medium heat, stirring constantly. Boil and stir for 1 minute. Remove from the heat. Add 1/2 cup of hot mixture into eggs; return to saucepan. Add sour cream and vanilla; beat with whisk until well blended. Place saucepan in a bowl of ice water for a few minutes to cool. Cover and chill. Serve sauce over berries. **Variation:** Strawberries or other fresh fruit may be substituted for raspberries. **Yield:** 6-8 servings.

DEFROSTING DO'S: To defrost frozen unbaked dough, transfer it from freezer to refrigerator for at least 8 hours before using. This gives the dough time to defrost gradually without absorbing excess moisture.

• To thaw an already baked dessert, remove it from the freezer to room temperature.

PARADISE PUDDING

Judith Snyder, Saxonburg, Pennsylvania

This recipe (like dumplings and sauce all in one!) was handed down from my husband's grandmother. It reminds my father of the delicious plum puddings he loved to eat as a little boy.

    2-1/2 cups water
        1 cup packed brown sugar
    CAKE:
        1 cup raisins
        1 cup all-purpose flour
        1 teaspoon butter *or* shortening
        1/2 cup packed brown sugar
        2 teaspoons baking powder
        1 teaspoon vanilla extract
        1/2 cup milk
        1/2 teaspoon ground cinnamon
        1/4 teaspoon ground nutmeg
        1/4 teaspoon salt

In a large skillet, bring water and brown sugar to a boil. Meanwhile, combine all cake ingredients in a large mixing bowl. Drop by tablespoonfuls into skillet. Reduce heat to low. Cover and simmer for about 1 hour. *Do not lift lid.* **Yield:** 8-10 servings.

STEAMED BREAD PUDDING

Ruth Samuels, Glendale, Arizona

Whenever I visited my grandma, this was the special dessert she fixed for me.

        1/4 cup butter *or* margarine, melted
        1 egg
        1 cup milk
        1/4 cup dark corn syrup
        1/4 cup packed brown sugar
        1/4 teaspoon baking soda
        1/4 teaspoon ground cloves
        1/2 teaspoon ground cinnamon
        1 cup raisins
        2 cups fine white bread crumbs
    LEMON SAUCE:
        1/2 cup butter *or* margarine
        3/4 cup sugar
        1/4 cup water
        1 egg, beaten
        3 tablespoons lemon juice
    Grated peel of 1 lemon

In the top of a 1-1/2-qt. double boiler, place melted butter; set aside. In a mixing bowl, combine egg, milk, corn syrup, sugar, baking soda and spices. Mix until smooth. Stir in raisins and crumbs. Pour over melted butter. Add at least 3 in. of water to bottom of double boiler; cover and steam over medium-low heat for 1-1/2 hours. Meanwhile, for sauce, combine butter, sugar, water, egg and lemon juice in a saucepan. Bring to a boil over medium heat, stirring constantly. Add lemon peel. Serve sauce hot over warm pudding. **Yield:** 6-8 servings.

LEMON CUSTARD PUDDING CAKE

Deborah Hill, Coffeyville, Kansas

(PICTURED ON PAGE 74)

This recipe originated in a 1949 cookbook that my mom had thrown out, but I fished out of the trash can and saved! I was only 10 at the time, but already had an interest in cooking. That little book is still a favorite of mine—and I own over 150 cookbooks!

        6 tablespoons all-purpose flour
        6 tablespoons butter *or* margarine, melted
        2 cups sugar, *divided*
        4 eggs, *separated*
    1-1/2 cups milk
    Grated peel of 1 lemon
        2 tablespoons fresh lemon juice
    Confectioners' sugar

In a large mixing bowl, combine flour, butter and 1-1/2 cups sugar. Beat egg yolks; add to mixing bowl along with milk and lemon peel. Mix well. Add lemon juice. In another bowl, beat egg whites until stiff, slowly adding remaining 1/2 cup sugar while beating. Fold into batter. Pour into a greased 2-qt. baking dish or individual ramekins. Place in a shallow pan of hot water and bake at 350° for 55-60 minutes or until lightly browned. Serve warm or chilled with confectioners' sugar dusted on top. **Yield:** 6-8 servings.

From Grandma's Kitchen: Vinegar Pie

"My grandmother created many of her own special recipes, including Vinegar Pie, which always turned out 100-percent good!"

When the air turns brisk and the apples begin to drop to the ground, Dora Williams pops a homemade Apple Cider Vinegar Pie into the oven, turns the oven to 350° and thinks back to the days when her grandmother first taught her to make that delicious pie—but under different circumstances.

"I lived with my parents on my grandparents' farm in Hicksville, Ohio during the Depression and my grandmother taught me to cook on an old wood-burning stove," says Dora, who now has seven grandchildren of her own. "We didn't have electricity or a furnace, and it was my duty to gather tree bark shavings and branches from the woods for kindling."

She also helped press and strain apples from their orchard to make and sell apple cider. Some of it was saved and kept cold in a big wooden barrel that was almost completely buried in the ground.

"On cold, crisp nights, Grandma would put fresh apple cider on the stove with a stick of cinnamon. Oh, it was so good!" Dora remembers. But even more memorable was when her grandmother would tie on an apron and announce, "Dora, let's make us a pie."

"My mouth would start watering and I'd say, 'Out of what, Grandma?'" Dora recalls. Times were tough, after all, yet her grandmother always managed to turn simple ingredients into scrumptious desserts. Some-

times she'd concoct creamy pies using buttermilk. This time, however, she used apple cider vinegar to bake the best pie that Dora had ever tasted.

Grandma's vinegar pies were also popular during threshing time, when all the local wives would join together and cook a feast for the harvesters, Dora reports.

"But before serving, Grandma would always give thanks. Having family devotions was number one in our household, and I guess having a good pie was number two," Dora says with a laugh.

Dora and her parents eventually moved to Laingsburg, Michigan, where she got married and raised six children. She never forgot her grandmother's Vinegar Pie, though…and neither do the folks who request it again and again at church and family gatherings.

VINEGAR PIE

4 eggs
1-1/2 cups sugar
1/4 cup butter *or* **margarine, melted**
1-1/2 tablespoons cider *or* **white vinegar**
1 teaspoon vanilla extract
1 unbaked pie shell (9 inches)

In a large bowl, combine eggs, sugar, butter, vinegar and vanilla. Mix well. Pour into pie shell. Bake at 350° for 45-50 minutes. **Yield:** 8 servings.

A Cook's Best-Kept Secret

What puts a shine on a pie crust minutes before it's done baking? Grandmothers of old knew that a touch of vinegar could do the job. In fact, vinegar was very handy for lots of other reasons, too.

Besides stirring up a vinegar pie that surpassed many lemon concoctions, old-time cooks used vinegar to tenderize meat, keep apples from turning brown and make bread and rolls crusty. A tablespoonful of vinegar used instead of cream of tartar made meringue beautifully high.

A little vinegar mixed into jugs of drinking water was considered more "cooling" for farmhands on hot days. As a cleansing agent, boiled vinegar and water kept lime deposits from forming on the inside of the teakettle, while a few tablespoons of vinegar added to a quart of water cleaned up rug stains. It also worked as a rinse for squeaky-clean hair, a preservative for pickling fruits and vegetables and a deodorant for food containers or fishy fry pans.

Perhaps you remember a few of your own secret uses for versatile vinegar!

STAR-SPANGLED SWEETS. Clockwise from bottom left: Lemon Custard Pudding Cake (p. 72), Golden Coconut Peach Pie (p. 77), Dutch Apple Pie (p. 78), Raspberries with Sour Cream Custard (p. 72), Strawberry Rhubarb Pie (p. 76).

DATE PUDDING CAKE
Evonne Wurmnest, Normal, Illinois

Anyone who likes dates will enjoy this rich date dessert. The recipe, which came out of my mother's old cookbook, is our favorite dessert for Thanksgiving, Christmas ...even New Year's gatherings.

1-1/2 cups packed brown sugar, *divided*
   3 tablespoons butter, *divided*
   1 cup all-purpose flour
   2 teaspoons baking powder
1/2 teaspoon salt
1/2 teaspoon ground cinnamon
1/2 cup chopped dates
1/2 cup chopped pecans
1/2 cup milk
   2 cups water
Whipped cream *or* ice cream

In a mixing bowl, cream 1/2 cup brown sugar and 1 tablespoon butter. Sift together flour, baking powder, salt and cinnamon; add dates and nuts. Add flour mixture alternately with milk to creamed mixture. Set aside. In a saucepan, combine water with remaining brown sugar and butter. Bring to a boil; boil 5 minutes. Pour into the bottom of a 9-in. round baking pan. Spoon batter on top of sauce. Bake at 350° for 45 minutes. Serve warm or cold with whipped cream or ice cream. **Yield:** 6-8 servings.

BUTTERSCOTCH PUDDING
Audrey Wall, Industry, Pennsylvania

Everyone always raves how much better this pudding tastes than the kind you make from a box.

   1 cup packed dark brown sugar
   4 tablespoons all-purpose flour
   2 eggs
1/8 teaspoon salt
   2 cups milk
   1 teaspoon vanilla extract

In a saucepan, combine sugar, flour, eggs, salt and milk. Cook over medium heat, stirring constantly, until mixture starts to bubble and thicken. Remove from heat. Blend in vanilla with hand beater. Pour into dessert cups and chill. **Yield:** 4 servings.

WHEN EGGS CAN'T BE BEAT. When whipping egg whites, make sure the beaters and the bowl are free of any greasy residue, or the whites won't whip.

● For more volume, let egg whites stand to room temperature before beating. Use a glass or metal bowl (not plastic) with a tapered bottom and a wide top. Egg whites expand six times when beaten, so be sure the bowl is large enough.

● To prevent yolks from mixing with the whites, separate eggs in small bowls before adding to your large mixing bowl.

ORANGE MERINGUE PIE
Callie Anne Miller, Destin, Florida

This light, luscious pie—my grandmother's specialty—is still one of our family's most-requested summertime desserts.

1-1/2 cups sugar
1/4 cup plus 2 tablespoons cornstarch
1/4 teaspoon salt
   3 cups orange juice
   4 egg yolks, well beaten
1/4 cup plus 2 tablespoons lemon juice
   3 tablespoons butter
1-1/2 teaspoons grated orange peel
   1 pie shell (9 inches), baked
MERINGUE:
   4 egg whites, room temperature
1/4 teaspoon cream of tartar
1/2 cup sugar

In a 2- to 3-qt. saucepan, combine sugar, cornstarch and salt. Using a wire whisk, gradually blend in orange juice until smooth. Add egg yolks and blend thoroughly. Add lemon juice and butter. Cook on medium heat, stirring constantly, and gradually bring to a boil. Reduce heat as mixture begins to thicken. Boil slowly for 1 minute. Remove from heat; stir in peel. Pour hot filling into pie shell. Let stand, allowing a thin film to form on top. Meanwhile, for meringue, beat egg whites in a small mixing bowl until foamy. Add cream of tartar; beat on high until soft peaks form. Reduce speed to medium; add sugar gradually, about 1 tablespoon at a time. Beat on high until stiff and glossy. Spoon meringue around edge of filling. Using a spatula, push meringue gently against inner edge of crust, sealing well. Swirl meringue into center of pie. Bake at 350° for 12-15 minutes or until meringue is golden brown. Cool on wire rack at room temperature for 2 hours before serving. To cut, use a sharp knife dipped in hot water. **Yield:** 8 servings.

STRAWBERRY RHUBARB PIE
Janice Schmidt, Baxter, Iowa
(PICTURED ON PAGE 75)

My niece tasted this pie at a family dinner and urged me to enter it in our hometown pie contest. She said it would win the Grand Prize, and she was right! I cook at our local nursing home and everyone enjoys this recipe.

   2 tablespoons cornstarch
   1 cup sugar
   1 cup water
   1 cup sliced rhubarb
1/2 3-ounce package strawberry-flavored gelatin
   2 pints fresh strawberries, halved
   1 pastry shell (9 inches), baked

In a medium saucepan, mix cornstarch and sugar. Stir in water until smooth. Add rhubarb; cook and stir until clear and thickened. Add gelatin and stir until dissolved. Cool. Pour about half of rhubarb sauce into pastry shell. Arrange berries over sauce; top with remaining sauce. Refrigerate 3-4 hours. **Yield:** 8 servings.

CHERRY BERRY PIE

Mamie Palmer, Sault Sainte Marie, Michigan
(PICTURED ON PAGE 68)

This good old recipe won first place in a pie-baking contest a few years ago, but it's been a winner in our family for generations!

>   1 can (16 ounces) pitted tart red cherries
>   1 package (10 ounces) frozen red raspberries, thawed
> 3/4 cup sugar
>   3 tablespoons cornstarch
>   3 tablespoons butter *or* margarine
> 1/4 teaspoon almond extract
> 1/4 teaspoon red food coloring
> **Pastry for double-crust pie (9 inches)**

Drain cherries and raspberries; reserve 1-1/4 cups juice and set fruit aside. In a saucepan, combine sugar and cornstarch; gradually stir in juice. Cook and stir over medium heat until the mixture begins to boil. Cook and stir 2 minutes longer. Remove from the heat; stir in butter, extract and food coloring. Gently fold in fruit. Cool slightly. Pour filling into pie crust and top with a lattice crust. Bake at 375° for 45 minutes or until bubbly. **Yield:** 8 servings.

Old-timers remember when a pie was set on the windowsill to cool—not to thaw!

GRANDMA'S SOUR CREAM RAISIN PIE

Beverly Medalen, Willow City, North Dakota
(PICTURED ON PAGE 68)

The aroma of this pie baking in my farm kitchen oven reminds me of my dear grandma who made this pretty pie for special occasions.

>   1 cup raisins
> 2/3 cup sugar
>   3 tablespoons cornstarch
> 1/8 teaspoon salt
> 1/8 teaspoon ground cloves
> 1/2 teaspoon ground cinnamon
>   1 cup (8 ounces) sour cream
>   3 egg yolks
> 1/2 cup milk
> 1/2 cup chopped nuts, optional
>   1 pie shell (9 inches), baked
> **MERINGUE:**
>   3 egg whites
> 1/4 teaspoon salt
>   5 tablespoons sugar

In a small saucepan, place raisins and enough water to cover; bring to a boil. Turn off heat; set aside. In a heavy saucepan, combine sugar, cornstarch, salt, cloves and cinnamon. Stir in sour cream. Beat in egg yolks. Add milk; cook over medium heat, stirring constantly, until pudding comes to a boil and is very thick. Remove from the heat.

Drain raisins, reserving 1/2 cup liquid. Stir liquid into filling. Add raisins, and nuts if desired. Pour into pie shell. For meringue, in a small mixing bowl, beat egg whites with salt until foamy. Gradually add sugar, about 1 tablespoon at a time; beat until stiff and glossy. Spread over pie, making sure meringue covers all of filling. Bake at 350° for 10-15 minutes or until light golden brown. Serve warm or cold. Store leftovers in the refrigerator. **Yield:** 8 servings.

SOUR CREAM RHUBARB PIE

Marcille Meyer, Battle Creek, Nebraska

Here's a pretty pie we make to celebrate the coming of summer each year.

>   4 cups cubed rhubarb
>   1 unbaked pie shell (10 inches)
>   2 eggs
> 1-1/2 cups sugar
>   1 cup (8 ounces) sour cream
>   3 tablespoons quick-cooking tapioca
> **Ground cinnamon**

Place rhubarb in pie shell. In a medium bowl, beat eggs. Add sugar, sour cream and tapioca. Pour over rhubarb. Sprinkle with cinnamon. Bake at 400° for 15 minutes. Reduce heat to 350° and continue baking for 30 minutes. **Yield:** 8-10 servings.

GOLDEN COCONUT PEACH PIE

Gloria Kratz, Des Moines, Iowa
(PICTURED ON PAGE 74)

This peaches-and-cream pie once captured the blue ribbon at the Iowa State Fair. It always disappears fast!

>   4 to 4-1/2 cups sliced fresh peaches
> 1/2 cup sugar
>   3 tablespoons all-purpose flour
> 1/4 teaspoon ground nutmeg
> 1/8 teaspoon salt
> 1/4 cup orange juice
>   1 unbaked pie shell (9 inches)
>   2 tablespoons butter
>   2 cups flaked coconut
>   1 can (5 ounces) evaporated milk
>   1 egg, beaten
> 1/4 to 1/2 cup sugar
> 1/4 teaspoon almond extract

In a medium bowl, combine peaches, sugar, flour, nutmeg, salt and juice. Pour into pie shell; dot with butter. Bake at 450° for 15 minutes. Meanwhile, combine remaining ingredients. Pour over hot filling. Reduce heat to 350° and bake until the coconut is toasted, about 40 minutes. Serve warm or chilled. Store in the refrigerator. **Yield:** 8 servings.

DUTCH APPLE PIE
Eugenia McQueen, Tampa, Florida
(PICTURED ON PAGE 74)

This delicious pie was brought to my mother's home the day after my father died on Christmas Eve 25 years ago. Every time I bake it I am reminded of the tremendous outpouring of love and support that we received. It's a pie that my sweet daddy would have loved!

> 3/4 cup sugar
> 2 tablespoons all-purpose flour
> Pinch salt
> 1 egg, beaten
> 1/2 teaspoon vanilla extract
> 1 cup (8 ounces) sour cream
> 2 cups chopped tart apples
> 1 unbaked pie shell (9 inches)
> STREUSEL TOPPING:
> 1/3 cup all-purpose flour
> 1/3 cup packed brown sugar
> 2 tablespoons butter

In a mixing bowl, combine sugar, flour and salt. Add egg, vanilla and sour cream; stir until smooth. Add apples; mix well. Pour into pie crust. Bake at 375° for 15 minutes. Reduce heat to 325° and bake for 30 minutes more. Meanwhile, for topping, combine flour and sugar. Cut in butter until crumbly. Sprinkle topping over pie; bake an additional 20 minutes. Serve warm or chilled. Store in the refrigerator. **Yield:** 8 servings.

LEMON MERINGUE PIE
Marie Hughes, Bedford, Kentucky

I think of my grandmother every time I make this pie...it's a recipe she made often. Because of my husband's engineering job, we've lived in several states, and I've shared this recipe with lots of friends I've made over the years.

> 1-1/2 cups sugar
> 6 tablespoons cornstarch
> Dash salt
> 1-1/2 cups water
> 3 egg yolks, lightly beaten
> 2 tablespoons butter *or* margarine
> 1/3 cup fresh lemon juice (about 3 lemons)
> 2 teaspoons grated lemon peel
> 1 pastry shell (9 inches), baked
> MERINGUE:
> 3 egg whites, room temperature
> 1/2 teaspoon vanilla extract
> 1/4 teaspoon cream of tartar
> 6 tablespoons sugar

In a saucepan, combine sugar, cornstarch and salt. Stir in water. Cook and stir over medium-high heat until thickened. Reduce heat; cook and stir 2 additional minutes. Gradually stir in 1 cup of hot filling to egg yolks; return to saucepan. Bring to a boil. Cook, stirring constantly, for 2 minutes. Remove from heat. Stir in butter, lemon juice and peel. Pour hot filling into pastry shell. For meringue, beat egg whites, vanilla and cream of tartar in a mixing bowl at medium speed until soft peaks form. Add sugar gradually, 1 tablespoon at a time, beating on high until stiff and glossy. Immediately spread over pie, sealing edges to pastry. Bake at 350° for 12-15 minutes or until meringue is golden. Cool. Store in refrigerator. **Yield:** 8 servings.

ALL-AMERICAN STRAWBERRY PIE
Ada Martin, Wellesley, Massachusetts

Sweet, red strawberries combined with pretty, tart blueberries, all layered atop a creamy vanilla pudding...that makes a red-white-and-blue pie that my grandmother would serve every Fourth of July!

> 3/4 cup sugar
> 1/2 cup all-purpose flour
> 1/4 teaspoon salt
> 3 cups milk
> 3 egg yolks, lightly beaten
> 2 tablespoons butter *or* margarine
> 1-1/2 teaspoons vanilla extract
> 1/2 pint heavy cream
> 1-1/2 tablespoons confectioners' sugar
> 1 pie shell (9 inches), baked
> 1 pint fresh strawberries, halved
> 1 cup fresh *or* frozen blueberries

In a 3-qt. saucepan, combine sugar, flour and salt. Add milk, stirring until smooth. Cook and stir over medium heat until thickened. Stir a small amount of milk mixture into yolks, then return all to saucepan. Cook, stirring, for 3 minutes. Remove from the heat; stir in butter and vanilla. Cool 20 minutes. Pour into pie shell; chill several hours until firm. Whip cream and sugar; spread half over pie filling. Arrange berries on cream. Dollop or pipe remaining cream around edge of pie. **Yield:** 8 servings.

MOM'S CRANBERRY PIE
Laura Belscher, Buffalo, New York

My family absolutely loves cranberries, especially in a pie. I've made this recipe for years and it's a must for the holidays.

> 2 cups fresh *or* frozen cranberries
> 1 to 1-1/2 cups sugar
> 2 tablespoons all-purpose flour
> 1 teaspoon vanilla extract
> 1/2 cup water
> 1 teaspoon grated orange peel, optional
> Pastry for a double-crust pie (9 inches)

In a large bowl, combine first six ingredients. Pour filling into pie shell and top with a lattice crust. Bake at 350° for 1 hour or until crust is golden brown. Cool. **Yield:** 8 servings.

AUTUMN ATTRACTIONS. On opposite page: Sweet Potato Pie (p. 81), Bread Pudding (p. 70).

PEACH PRALINE PIE
Elizabeth Hunter, Prosperity, South Carolina

Peach pie is typical of our state, and this recipe includes typically Southern praline topping. It was given to me when I married and set up our home more than 40 years ago. I can and freeze peaches to make this pie year-round.

> 4 cups sliced peeled ripe peaches
>   (about 3 pounds)
> 1/2 cup sugar
> 2 tablespoons quick-cooking tapioca
> 1 teaspoon lemon juice
> 1/2 cup all-purpose flour
> 1/4 cup packed brown sugar
> 1/2 cup chopped pecans
> 1/4 cup butter *or* margarine
> 1 unbaked deep-dish pie shell (9 inches)

In a large bowl, combine peaches, sugar, tapioca and lemon juice; let stand 15 minutes. Meanwhile, combine flour, brown sugar and pecans in a small bowl; cut in butter until crumbly. Sprinkle 1/3 of crumbs over bottom of pie shell; cover with peach mixture. Sprinkle remaining crumbs on top, allowing peaches to show if desired. Bake at 450° for 10 minutes. Reduce heat to 350° and bake 20 minutes longer or until peaches are tender and topping is golden brown. **Yield:** 8-10 servings.

Sunday-Go-to-Eatin'

Every Sunday when I was growing up, we had dinner at the Grandmas'. This meant a noon meal at Grandma Fannie's and an evening meal at Grandma Hood's.

I wouldn't have missed any of them for the world! Each meal was truly a feast, aimed to serve a large crowd of aunts, uncles and cousins.

Naturally, no meal was complete without dessert, so there was always an array of cakes, pies or cobblers to leave room for. Back then, both of my grandmas used lard or even bacon grease instead of shortening, and their desserts always looked and tasted wonderful!

—*Peggy Spieckermann, Washington, Iowa*

CHOCOLATE PECAN PIE
Sharon Claussen, Wheat Ridge, Colorado

Here's a nice variation of a rich, old-fashioned pecan pie that's a breeze to make.

> 3 eggs, lightly beaten
> 1 cup light *or* dark corn syrup
> 1/2 cup sugar
> 1/2 cup semisweet chocolate chips
> 2 tablespoons butter *or* margarine, melted

> 1 teaspoon vanilla extract
> 1-1/2 cups pecan halves
> 1 unbaked pastry shell (9 inches)

In a large bowl, combine eggs, corn syrup, sugar, chips, butter and vanilla until well blended. Stir in pecans. Pour into pastry shell. Bake at 350° for about 50 minutes or until knife inserted near center comes out clean. **Yield:** 8 servings.

OZARK BLUEBERRY PIE
Doris Hay, Kimberling City, Missouri

Blueberries grow well in this area, and this old-time recipe goes over well with pie eaters. It won first prize at the 1990 Missouri State Fair!

FILLING:
> 1 can (16 ounces) whole-berry cranberry sauce
> 1/3 cup packed brown sugar
> 1/4 cup sugar
> 2 tablespoons all-purpose flour
> 2 tablespoons cornstarch
> 2 tablespoons orange juice
> 1/2 teaspoon grated orange peel
> 1/8 teaspoon salt
> 2 cups fresh *or* frozen blueberries

CRUST:
> 2-2/3 cups all-purpose flour
> 1 teaspoon salt
> 1/2 teaspoon ground mace
> 1 cup shortening
> 6 tablespoons ice water
> 2 tablespoons butter
> 1 egg
> 1 tablespoon water

In a large bowl, combine first eight filling ingredients. Stir in blueberries; set aside. For crust, combine flour, salt and mace in another bowl. Cut in shortening until mixture is in pea-size chunks. Add ice water, 1 tablespoon at a time, and toss lightly with a fork until dough forms a ball. Divide dough in half. On a floured surface and using a floured rolling pin, roll one half to a 10-in. circle. Place into 9-in. pie pan. Spoon filling into crust; dot with butter. Roll second half of dough to fit top of pie. Moisten edge of bottom crust; place top crust over. Fold edge under bottom crust; flute with fingers. Beat egg with water; brush over crust. Cut slits in top. Bake at 425° for 40 minutes or until golden brown. **Yield:** 8 servings.

SWEET POTATO PIE
Shari Millican, Smyrna, Georgia
(PICTURED ON PAGE 79)

I first tried this delicious pie at a church potluck dinner and was immediately hooked. I've spent many years perfecting my own recipe.

1-1/4 cups sugar
1/2 teaspoon ground cinnamon
1/2 teaspoon ground nutmeg
2 eggs
1 can (12 ounces) evaporated milk
1 teaspoon vanilla extract
1-1/2 cups mashed cooked sweet potatoes
1 unbaked pie crust (9 inches)
TOPPING:
1/3 cup butter *or* margarine
1/3 cup all-purpose flour
1/2 cup packed brown sugar
1/2 cup shredded coconut
1/2 cup chopped pecans

Whipped cream *or* ice cream

In a mixing bowl, blend sugar and spices. In another bowl, beat eggs; add milk and vanilla. Combine with sugar mixture. Stir in potatoes; beat until smooth. Pour into pie shell. Bake at 425° for 15 minutes. Reduce heat to 350° and bake an additional 30 minutes. Meanwhile, combine topping ingredients. Sprinkle on pie; return to the oven for 10-15 minutes or until topping is golden brown. Cool on a wire rack. Serve with whipped cream or ice cream. Store in refrigerator. **Yield:** 6-8 servings. **Variation:** For pumpkin pie, substitute equal amounts of canned or mashed cooked pumpkin for the 1-1/2 cups mashed cooked sweet potatoes.

APPLE PIE
Maggie Greene, Granite Falls, Washington
(PICTURED ON OUR COVER)

I remember coming home sullen one day because we'd lost a softball game. Grandma, in her wisdom, suggested, "Maybe a slice of hot apple pie will make you feel better." One bite...and Grandma was right.

1/2 cup sugar
1/2 cup packed brown sugar
3 tablespoons all-purpose flour
1 teaspoon ground cinnamon
1/4 teaspoon ground ginger
1/4 teaspoon ground nutmeg
7 to 8 cups thinly sliced pared apples
1 tablespoon lemon juice
Pastry for double-crust pie (9 inches)
1 tablespoon butter *or* margarine
1 egg white
Additional sugar

In a small bowl, combine sugars, flour and spices; set aside. In a large bowl, toss apples with lemon juice. Add sugar mixture; toss well to coat. Line a 9-in. pie pan with half the pastry. Place apple filling into crust; dot with butter. Roll out remaining pastry to fit top of pie. Cut a few slits in top. Beat egg white until foamy; brush over pastry. Sprinkle sugar on top. Bake at 375° for 35 minutes. Increase temperature to 400° and bake 10-15 minutes more or until golden. **Yield:** 8 servings.

INGREDIENT SUBSTITUTIONS

For:	Substitute:
1 cup corn syrup	1 cup sugar plus 1/4 cup liquid*
1 cup honey	1-1/4 cups sugar plus 1/4 cup liquid*
1 ounce chocolate	3 tablespoons cocoa plus 1 tablespoon fat
1 cup buttermilk or sour milk	1 tablespoon vinegar *or* lemon juice plus enough sweet milk to make 1 cup (let stand 5 minutes) or 1-3/4 teaspoons cream of tartar plus 1 cup sweet milk

(*whatever liquid is called for in the recipe)

GRANDMA'S CHOCOLATE MERINGUE PIE
Donna Vest Tilley, Chesterfield, Virginia

My grandmother served chocolate meringue pie after Sunday dinner each week, usually with an apology it was "too runny" or something else was wrong with it. Of course, it was never less than perfect!

3/4 cup sugar
5 tablespoons baking cocoa
3 tablespoons cornstarch
1/4 teaspoon salt
2 cups milk
3 egg yolks, beaten
1 teaspoon vanilla extract
1 pie shell (9 inches), baked
MERINGUE:
3 egg whites
1/4 teaspoon cream of tartar
6 tablespoons sugar

In a saucepan, mix sugar, cocoa, cornstarch and salt; gradually add milk. Cook and stir over medium-high heat until thickened and bubbly. Reduce heat; cook and stir 2 minutes more. Remove from heat. Stir about 1 cup of the hot filling into the egg yolks. Return to the saucepan and bring to a gentle boil. Cook and stir for 2 minutes. Remove from heat and stir in vanilla. Pour hot filling into pie crust. For meringue, immediately beat egg whites with cream of tartar until soft peaks form. Gradually add sugar, about 1 tablespoon at a time, and continue to beat until stiff and glossy. Spread evenly over filling, sealing meringue to crust. Bake at 350° for 12-15 minutes or until golden. **Yield:** 8 servings.

OATMEAL PIE
Ruth Gritter, Grand Rapids, Michigan

This delicious pie recipe came from my mother. My husband especially enjoys it during the holidays. I have shared the pie crust with many others because it's flaky and so easy to roll out. We even use it at our children's school when apple pies are made for a fund-raiser.

    1/2 cup sugar
    1/2 cup light *or* dark corn syrup
    3/4 cup rolled oats
    1/2 cup coconut
    1/2 cup butter *or* margarine, melted
    2 eggs, well beaten
    1 teaspoon vanilla extract
    1 unbaked Never-Fail Pie Crust (recipe below)
    1 package (3 ounces) pecan halves

In a large bowl, combine sugar, corn syrup, oats, coconut, butter, eggs and vanilla. Pour into crust. Bake at 350° for 15-20 minutes. Arrange pecans on top of pie; bake 30 minutes more or until well browned. **Yield:** 8 servings.

NEVER-FAIL PIE CRUST

    2 cups all-purpose flour
    1 teaspoon salt
    2/3 cup shortening
    1/3 cup milk
    1 tablespoon vinegar

Combine flour and salt in a mixing bowl. Cut in shortening. Add milk and vinegar. Shape dough into a ball. Chill for 30 minutes. Divide dough in half. On a lightly floured surface, roll out each half to fit a 9-in. pie pan. **Yield:** 2 9-inch crusts.

GERMAN CHOCOLATE PIE
Crystal Allen, Homer, Illinois

This chocolate pie has been a holiday tradition in our family for generations, and it's just as popular now as when my grandmother made it years ago!

    1 package (4 ounces) German sweet chocolate
    1/4 cup butter
    1 can (12 ounces) evaporated milk
1-1/2 cups sugar
    3 tablespoons cornstarch

    1/8 teaspoon salt
    2 eggs
    1 teaspoon vanilla extract
    1 unbaked deep-dish pie shell (9 inches)
1-1/2 cups coconut
    1 cup pecans, chopped

In a saucepan, combine chocolate and butter. Melt over low heat. Remove from the heat and blend in milk; set aside. In a mixing bowl, combine sugar, cornstarch and salt. Beat in eggs and vanilla. Blend in melted chocolate; pour into pie shell. Combine coconut and pecans; sprinkle on top of pie. Bake at 375° for 45 minutes. **Yield:** 8-10 servings.

MAMA ARNOLD'S HONEY PIE
Ruth Arnold, Pearsall, Texas

My mother developed this recipe, which was my father's longtime favorite dessert (he lived to be 104!).

    1 cup honey
    3 eggs, beaten
    3 tablespoons butter
    1 teaspoon vanilla extract
    1 cup chopped pecans
Dash nutmeg
    1 unbaked pie shell (9 inches)

In a saucepan, bring honey to a boil. Quickly beat in eggs. Add butter, vanilla, pecans and nutmeg. Pour into pie shell. Bake at 325° for 25 minutes or until set. **Yield:** 6-8 servings.

LEMON CLOUD PIE
Katherine Painter, San Francisco, California

This flavorful, festive pie is my favorite for parties and family gatherings.

MERINGUE SHELL:
    4 egg whites
    1/2 teaspoon cream of tartar
    1/4 teaspoon salt
    1/2 teaspoon vanilla extract
    1 cup sugar
LEMON FILLING:
    4 egg yolks
    1/2 cup sugar
    3 tablespoons lemon juice
Peel of 1 lemon
Dash salt
    1 cup heavy cream, whipped
Additional whipped cream and lemon slices, optional

In a mixing bowl, beat egg whites with cream of tartar, salt and vanilla until soft peaks form. Add sugar gradually, about 1 tablespoon at a time, and beat until very stiff. Place in a greased 9-in. baking dish. Bake at 275° for 55 minutes, or until meringue is a light cream color and is dry and firm to the touch. Cool thoroughly. For filling, beat egg yolks in the top of a double boiler. Add sugar, lemon juice, peel and salt. Cook until thick, about 5-8 minutes. Cool. Fold in whipped cream. Spoon into shell. Refrigerate overnight. If desired, garnish with whipped cream and lemon slices. **Yield:** 8-10 servings.

≈❤❤❤≈

PECAN PIE
Virginia Jung, Janesville, Wisconsin

This pie was always a favorite for birthdays while my children were growing up. They never liked the typical party cakes. My mother gave me the old-fashioned recipe for lard crust...it turns out every time!

    4 eggs
    1 cup sugar
    1/8 teaspoon salt
1-1/2 cups dark corn syrup
    2 tablespoons plus 1 teaspoon butter, melted
        and cooled
    1 teaspoon vanilla extract
    1 cup pecan halves
    1 unbaked Lard Pie Crust (recipe below)

In a mixing bowl, beat eggs just until blended but not frothy. Add sugar, salt and corn syrup. Add butter and vanilla, mixing just enough to blend. Spread pecans in the bottom of pie shell. Pour in filling. Place in a 350° oven and immediately reduce heat to 325°. Bake for 50-60 minutes. **Yield:** 8-10 servings.

MOM'S LARD PIE CRUST

1-1/2 cups all-purpose flour
Pinch salt
    1/2 cup lard
    3 to 4 tablespoons cold water

In a mixing bowl, combine flour and salt. Cut in lard until mixture resembles coarse crumbs. Sprinkle in water, a tablespoon at a time, until pastry holds together. Shape into a ball; chill for 30 minutes. On a lightly floured surface, roll dough to 1/8-in. thickness. Transfer to a 10-in. pie plate. Flute edges; fill and bake as pie recipe directs. **Yield:** 1 10-inch crust.

≈❤≈

Practice Makes Perfect

Grandmother was trying to teach little Tommy some table manners. After a few lessons, he said, "Grandmother, you said I should always eat my pie with a fork when I am invited out to dinner."

"Yes, that's right," his grandmother replied.

"Well," Tommy said, "do you have a piece of pie that I could practice on?"

—Sally Koch, Poynette, Wisconsin

≈❤❤❤≈

OLD-TIME BUTTERMILK PIE
Kate Mathews, Shreveport, Louisiana

This recipe is older than I am...and I was born in 1919! My mother and grandmother made this pie with buttermilk and eggs from our farm and set it on the tables at church meetings and social gatherings. I did the same and now our children make it, too!

CRUST:
1-1/2 cups all-purpose flour
    1 teaspoon salt
    1/2 cup shortening
    1/4 cup cold milk
    1 egg, beaten
FILLING:
    1/2 cup butter *or* margarine
    2 cups sugar
    3 tablespoons all-purpose flour
    3 eggs
    1 cup buttermilk
    1 teaspoon vanilla extract
    1 teaspoon ground cinnamon
    1/4 cup lemon juice

In a bowl, mix flour and salt. Cut in shortening until smooth. Gradually add milk and egg; blend well. On a floured board, roll dough out very thin. Place in a 10-in. pie pan; set aside. For filling, cream butter and sugar in a mixing bowl. Add flour. Add eggs, one at a time, beating well after each addition. Stir in remaining ingredients and mix well. Pour into crust. Bake at 350° for 45 minutes. Cool completely before serving. **Yield:** 8-10 servings.

≈❤❤❤≈

PEANUT BUTTER PIE
Joan Wallace, Winchester, Kansas

This rich, old-fashioned dessert was an immediate hit with three girlfriends I used to live with. Now my husband and I run a small church camp and our two boys consume a lot of our time and energy—as well as my peanut butter pie!

    1 cup confectioners' sugar
    1/2 cup creamy peanut butter
    1 pie shell (9 inches), baked
    3 eggs, *separated*
    1/4 cup cornstarch
    2/3 cup sugar
    1/4 teaspoon salt
    2 cups milk
    3 tablespoons butter
    1/4 teaspoon vanilla extract

Place confectioners' sugar in a bowl. Cut in the peanut butter with a pastry blender until crumbly. Spread half of mixture in pie shell. In the top of a double boiler, beat egg yolks. In another bowl, combine cornstarch, sugar and salt; add milk and mix well. Pour over egg yolks; cook until mixture thickens. Add butter and vanilla; cook and stir until butter melts. Pour into pie shell. In a small bowl, beat the egg whites until stiff. Spread evenly over filling. Sprinkle remaining peanut butter mixture on top. Bake at 325° for 10-15 minutes or until golden brown. **Yield:** 8-10 servings.

Quick & Easy

"How can a dessert that's so easy to prepare taste so good?"

THEY say "necessity is the mother of invention"—and our mothers and grandmothers often found it necessary to invent quick and easy desserts to please their loved ones' sweet tooth.

With few dessert ingredients in the pantry, and little time between chores, child-rearing and meal preparation, old-time cooks learned to improvise when it came to dessert. From Flourless Peanut Butter Cookies and Chocolate Whipped Cream Cake to Lemonade Pie, Grandma concocted simple but unique desserts that, once tasted, deserved to be duplicated.

Today, Grandma's speedy old standbys can still satisfy a family's hankering for something sweet—without sacrificing taste or taking much time to prepare. So next time you need a great dessert in a hurry, try one of the fast, no-fuss desserts in this chapter. They're all delicious!

CHOCOLATE CHIP CAKE
Amy Heberer, Savoy, Illinois

It's hard to believe this wonderfully moist chocolate cake starts with a cake mix and is so easy to make!

  1 box (18-1/4 ounces) yellow cake mix
  1 package (3.4 ounces) instant vanilla
    pudding mix
  4 eggs
  1 cup (8 ounces) sour cream
1/2 cup vegetable oil
  1 cup water
  1 package (4 ounces) German sweet
    chocolate, grated
  1 cup (6 ounces) regular *or* miniature
    chocolate chips
  1 cup chopped pecans
Vanilla ice cream, optional

In a large mixing bowl, combine cake and pudding mixes, eggs, sour cream, oil and water. Beat until well blended and creamy. Stir in chocolate and nuts by hand. Spread evenly into a greased and floured 10-in. tube pan. Bake at 350° for 1 hour and 10 minutes or until a toothpick inserted in center of cake comes out clean. Cool. Slice into thin pieces and serve with a scoop of ice cream if desired. **Yield:** 12-16 servings.

TIME-TESTED TREATS. Opposite page, top to bottom: Yogurt Lemon Pie, Aunt Marion's Fruit Salad Dessert (p. 86), Strawberry Mousse (right).

LEMON REFRIGERATOR CAKE
June Mullins, Livonia, Missouri

This recipe comes from my church group and is a light, refreshing cake for warm-weather days.

  1 box (18-1/4 ounces) white cake mix
  1 package (3 ounces) cook and serve lemon
    pudding mix
Grated peel and juice of 1 lemon
  1 cup evaporated milk, chilled
1/4 cup sugar
  1 cup shredded coconut, *divided*

Prepare and bake cake according to package directions, using a greased and floured 13-in. x 9-in. x 2-in. baking pan. Cool in pan 10 minutes before removing to a wire rack. Prepare pudding according to package directions. Add lemon peel; cool. In a small bowl, whip milk. Add lemon juice and sugar; blend for 30 seconds. Fold into pudding. Carefully fold in 3/4 cup coconut. Split cooled cake into two layers; spread pudding mixture between layers and on top. Sprinkle with remaining coconut. Store in refrigerator. **Yield:** 12-15 servings.

STRAWBERRY MOUSSE
Callie Rose McClaine, Rainbow, Texas
(PICTURED ON PAGE 84)

Lightly sweet and refreshing, this easy-to-make mousse is a family favorite!

CRUST:
1/2 cup butter, softened
1/4 cup confectioners' sugar
  1 cup all-purpose flour
FILLING:
  2 pints fresh strawberries, *divided*
  2 tablespoons lemon juice
3/4 cup sugar
  2 envelopes unflavored gelatin
1/4 cup water
  2 cups whipping cream, whipped
Few drops red food coloring, optional

In a mixing bowl, cream butter and sugar. With a fork, stir in flour. Pat into the bottom of a 9-in. or 10-in. springform pan; prick with a fork. Bake at 350° for 10 minutes. Reduce heat to 300° and bake 20-25 minutes longer or until golden. Cool. Meanwhile, for filling, puree enough berries (about 1-1/2 pints) to make 2 cups. Reserve remaining berries for garnish. Blend lemon juice and sugar into puree. Combine gelatin and water in a saucepan; warm over low heat to dissolve. Add gelatin to puree; chill until mixture begins to thicken. Fold in whipped cream, and food coloring if desired. Pour into crust; chill. Garnish with reserved berries. **Yield:** 8-10 servings.

YOGURT LEMON PIE
Elsie Culver, Big Arm, Montana
(PICTURED ON PAGE 84)

This tasty recipe came about by experimenting in my kitchen. I'm a 75-year-old grandmother and great-grandmother, and when I'm not baking for relatives or friends, I'm busy tending my cherry orchard or skiing, bowling or dancing!

    1/3 cup milk
    1 package (8 ounces) cream cheese, softened
    2 cups plain yogurt
    1 package (3.4 ounces) instant lemon
      pudding mix
    1 pastry shell *or* graham cracker crust
      (9 inches), baked and cooled
Whipped topping, optional
Lemon peel, cut into thin strips, optional

In a mixing bowl, beat milk and cream cheese until smooth. Stir in yogurt until smooth. Add pudding mix and blend until mixture begins to thicken. Spoon into crust. Serve immediately or refrigerate until serving time. If desired, garnish with whipped topping and lemon peel strips. **Yield:** 8-10 servings.

AUNT MARION'S FRUIT SALAD DESSERT
Marion LaTourette, Honesdale, Pennsylvania
(PICTURED ON PAGE 84)

Aunt Marion, my namesake, is like a grandma to me. She gave me this luscious salad recipe, which goes to all our family reunions, hunt club suppers and snowmobile club picnics...and I go home with no leftovers!

    1 can (11 ounces) mandarin oranges*, drained
    1 can (20 ounces) pineapple chunks*, drained
    1 can (16 ounces) sliced peaches*, drained, cut
      into bite-size pieces
    3 bananas, sliced
    2 unpeeled red apples, cut into bite-size pieces
FRUIT SAUCE:
    1 package (3.4 ounces) instant vanilla
      pudding mix
    1 cup cold milk
    1/3 cup frozen orange juice concentrate, thawed
      and undiluted
    3/4 cup sour cream

In a large bowl, combine all fruit. Mix together gently; set aside. For sauce, combine all ingredients in another large bowl. Beat with a wire whisk until smooth (mixture will thicken). Gently fold fruit into sauce. Cover and chill for 3-4 hours before serving. (*Fresh fruit may be substituted for canned.) **Yield:** 10 servings (2 quarts).

SPEEDY APPLE CRISP
Lucy Euvrard, Okena, Ohio

My husband says he married me for my apple pie, but this recipe is much quicker to make. It's delicious by itself or topped with ice cream.

    5 to 6 cups sliced peeled baking apples
    1/2 cup all-purpose flour
    1/2 cup rolled oats
    3/4 cup packed brown sugar
    1/2 to 1 teaspoon ground cinnamon
    1/3 cup butter *or* margarine

Spread apples in a 9-in. square baking pan. Combine flour, oats, sugar and cinnamon in a bowl; cut in butter until mixture resembles coarse crumbs. Sprinkle over apples. Bake at 375° for 30-35 minutes or until apples are tender and topping is golden. Serve warm. **Yield:** 6-8 servings.

FREEZE-AHEAD PEACH PIE FILLING
Mary Ellen Thomas, Greer, South Carolina

This recipe makes four of the best, juiciest pies around!

    4 quarts sliced peeled fresh peaches
3-1/2 cups sugar
    3/4 cup quick-cooking tapioca
    3/4 teaspoon salt
    1/4 cup lemon juice

In a large mixing bowl, combine all ingredients. Let stand for 15 minutes. Line four 9-in. pie pans with foil. Spoon fruit mixture into pans and level. Place in freezer until frozen solid. When frozen, close foil, sealing well to prevent freezer burn. Remove foil from pans and freeze until ready to use. **To bake:** Remove frozen peaches from foil and place in a unbaked pastry shell. Cover with top crust and seal; brush top with melted butter. Cover crust edges with foil. Bake at 400° for 50 minutes. Remove foil and bake 20 minutes more or until crust is golden brown and filling is bubbly. **Yield:** recipe makes enough filling for 4 pies.

LEMON CHEESE BARS
Doris Dobbs, Canton, Ohio

These tart and crunchy lemon bars are a hit at family picnics, church suppers and in field lunches. They're easy to bake and to carry.

    1 box (18-1/4 ounces) yellow cake mix
    2 eggs, *divided*
    1/3 cup vegetable oil
    1 package (8 ounces) cream cheese, softened
    1/3 cup sugar
    1 tablespoon lemon juice

In a large bowl, combine cake mix, 1 egg and oil; stir until crumbly. Reserve 1 cup and press remaining mixture into an ungreased 13-in. x 9-in. x 2-in. baking pan. Bake at 350° for 15 minutes. In another bowl, beat cream cheese, sugar, lemon juice and remaining egg until fluffy. Spread over cake. Sprinkle with reserved cake mixture. Bake for another 15 minutes. Cool. **Yield:** 48 bars.

QUICK CHOCOLATE MOUSSE
Elsie Shell, Topeka, Indiana

This recipe is especially convenient when unexpected guests arrive. It's so easy to whip up and looks pretty with a mint leaf garnish.

> 1 can (14 ounces) sweetened condensed milk
> 1 package (3.9 ounces) instant chocolate
>   pudding mix
> 1 cup cold water
> 1 cup whipping cream, whipped
Additional whipped cream

In a large mixing bowl, combine milk, pudding mix and water. Beat until well mixed. Chill for 5 minutes. Fold in whipped cream. Spoon into individual serving dishes. Garnish with additional whipped cream. **Yield:** 4-6 servings.

ORANGE CREME SQUARES
Loreen Mezei, Medicine Hat, Alberta

This recipe may tempt you to skip supper and go straight to dessert! It was passed from my grandmother to my mom and is now a favorite of mine...as well as my husband's—he can't get enough of it! I often double the recipe, since it never lasts long.

CRUST:
> 3/4 cup graham cracker crumbs
> 1/4 cup lightly packed brown sugar
> 1/4 cup butter *or* margarine, melted
FILLING:
> 3/4 cup cold milk
> 1 pint vanilla ice cream, softened
> 2 teaspoons grated orange peel
> 1 package (3.4 ounces) instant vanilla
>   pudding mix
GLAZE:
> 4 teaspoons cornstarch
> 1/4 cup sugar
> 1/2 cup orange juice
> 2 tablespoons lemon juice
> 1 can (11 ounces) mandarin oranges, juice
>   drained and reserved

Combine crust ingredients and press into an 8-in. square pan. Chill. For filling, combine milk, ice cream and orange peel in a mixing bowl. Add pudding mix, beating slowly with rotary beater or at lowest speed of a mixer until well blended. Pour over crust. Chill until set, about 1 hour. Meanwhile, for glaze, combine cornstarch, sugar, orange juice, lemon juice and reserved mandarin orange juice in a saucepan. Bring to a boil. Reduce heat and cook, stirring constantly, until mixture thickens, about 2 minutes. Remove from the heat and cool. Arrange oranges on top of filling. Spoon glaze over top. Chill until set. **Yield:** 9 servings.

FAST FROZEN FRUIT: Keep grated orange and lemon peels handy for baking by preparing them ahead and freezing in small containers.

ORANGE FRUIT DIP
Vicki Eatwell, Eau Claire, Wisconsin

Served with fresh fruit, this dip makes a delicious appetizer that won't spoil appetites.

> 1 package (8 ounces) cream cheese, softened
> 1 cup marshmallow creme
Grated peel of 1 orange

Combine all ingredients and mix well. Refrigerate. Serve with fresh fruit, such as grapes, apple or pear slices, or pineapple or melon chunks. Dip apple and pear slices in orange or lemon juice before serving to prevent browning.

CRANBERRY CAKE RING
Darlene Muller, Pipestone, Minnesota

This beautiful fruit and nut cake ring mixes tart red cranberries with spicy mace for a unique taste.

> 1 package (3 ounces) cream cheese, softened
> 1 box (18-1/4 ounces) lemon cake mix
> 3/4 cup milk
> 4 eggs
> 1-1/4 cups ground cranberries
> 1/2 cup nuts, broken
> 1/4 cup sugar
> 1/2 to 1 teaspoon ground mace

In a large mixing bowl, place cream cheese, cake mix and milk; beat for 2 minutes. Add eggs; beat 2 minutes longer. Combine remaining ingredients; fold into batter. Pour into a greased and floured 10-in. tube pan. Bake at 350° for 1 hour. Remove from pan and cool on a wire rack. **Yield:** 16-20 servings.

TURTLE NUT CAKE
Freida Miller, Benton Harbor, Michigan
(PICTURED ON PAGE 89)

One of my cousins served this at our annual family reunion many years ago, and she was swamped with recipe requests. One taste will tell you why!

> 1 box (18-1/4 ounces) German chocolate
>   cake mix
> 1 package (14 ounces) caramels
> 1/2 cup evaporated milk
> 6 tablespoons butter *or* margarine
> 1 cup chopped pecans
> 1 cup (6 ounces) chocolate chips
Pecan halves for garnish, optional

Prepare cake according to package directions. Set aside half of batter; pour remaining batter into a greased and floured 13-in. x 9-in. x 2-in. baking pan. Bake at 350° for 18 minutes. Meanwhile, in a saucepan, melt caramels, milk and butter. Remove from heat; add nuts. Pour over cake. Sprinkle with chocolate chips, then pour reserved batter over top. Bake 20 minutes more or until cake springs back when touched lightly. Cool. Cut into squares and top each with a pecan half if desired. **Yield:** 20 servings.

FLOURLESS PEANUT BUTTER COOKIES
Maggie Schimmel, Wauwatosa, Wisconsin
(PICTURED ON PAGE 89)

When my mother (who's now a great-grandmother) gave me this recipe about 15 years ago, I was skeptical, because it calls for only three ingredients and no flour. But since then I've never had a failure, and I make them all the time!

> 1 egg, beaten
> 1 cup sugar
> 1 cup creamy peanut butter

In a large bowl, mix all ingredients. Roll level tablespoons into balls. Place on an ungreased cookie sheet; flatten with a fork. Bake at 350° for about 18 minutes. Remove to a wire rack to cool. **Yield:** 2 dozen.

The Cookie Jar

My mother had a cookie jar
Upon the pantry shelf.
Whenever I'd get hungry,
I'd go and help myself.

Until one day at dinner
When I didn't feel like eating.
She checked the cookie jar
And found it was depleting.

My mother hid that cookie jar
From me and everyone.
And now she passes treats around
After dinner's done!

RASPBERRY/LIME PIE
Jane Zemple, Midland, Michigan

This pie mixes up fast, and the raspberries give it a unique flavor! It's also appealing to the eye.

> 1 can (14 ounces) sweetened condensed milk
> 1/2 cup lime juice
> 1 carton (8 ounces) frozen whipped topping, thawed
> Few drops red food coloring, optional
> 1 cup fresh raspberries
> 1 graham cracker pie crust (9 inches), baked and cooled
> Raspberries for garnish
> Fresh mint leaves for garnish

In a mixing bowl, stir together milk and lime juice (mixture will begin to thicken). Mix in whipped topping. Add food coloring if desired. Gently fold in raspberries. Spoon into pie crust. Chill. Garnish with raspberries and mint. **Yield:** 8 servings.

LEMON CREAM TORTE
Eleanor Grofvert, Kalamazoo, Michigan

Although my husband has retired from farming, I haven't retired from the kitchen! I still enjoy cooking and preparing our children's old favorites as well as trying new recipes. The creamy texture and lemony flavor of this dessert give the taste buds a treat!

> 1/2 cup butter *or* margarine
> 1-1/4 cups all-purpose flour
> 1 package (8 ounces) cream cheese, softened
> 1 cup confectioners' sugar
> 1 carton (8 ounces) frozen whipped topping, thawed, *divided*
> 2 packages (3.4 ounces *each*) instant lemon pudding mix
> 2-1/2 cups cold milk
> 1/2 cup chopped pecans, optional

Combine butter and flour; pat into a 13-in. x 9-in. x 2-in. baking pan. Bake at 350° for 20-25 minutes or until lightly browned. Cool. In a large mixing bowl, blend cream cheese and sugar on medium speed until smooth. Add half of the whipped topping, beating on low. Spread over crust. In another bowl, beat pudding mixes and milk for 2 minutes on low speed. Let set 10 minutes. Spread over cream cheese layer; let set 10-15 minutes. Cover with remaining whipped topping. Top with pecans if desired. Refrigerate overnight. **Yield:** 16 servings.

CRUNCHY-TOP GINGERBREAD
Karen Templeton, Montrose, Pennsylvania
(PICTURED ON PAGE 89)

My grandmother often served this dessert with her special Sunday dinners, and my mother and I have also taken it to church suppers over the years. I love baking and I usually fall asleep reading cookbooks in bed.

> 1 package (14-1/2 ounces) gingerbread mix
> 1/4 cup packed brown sugar
> 2 tablespoons all-purpose flour
> 2 tablespoons butter *or* margarine
> 1/8 teaspoon salt
> 1 teaspoon ground cinnamon
> 1/2 cup chopped walnuts
> Whipped topping, optional

Prepare gingerbread according to package directions. Bake in a greased 11-in. x 7-in. baking pan at 350° for 25 minutes. Meanwhile, in a mixing bowl, combine brown sugar, flour, butter, salt, cinnamon and nuts; mix well. Sprinkle over gingerbread; bake for an additional 10 minutes. Cut into squares and serve warm. Garnish with a dollop of whipped topping if desired. **Yield:** 12-15 servings.

SPEEDY SNACKS. Opposite page, top to bottom: Flourless Peanut Butter Cookies (above), Turtle Nut Cake (p. 87), Crunchy-Top Gingerbread (above).

DANISH CHRISTMAS CAKE
Geraldine Nelson, River Falls, Wisconsin

This festive cake slices into beautiful torte-like layers—just right for the holidays.

    1 box (18-1/4 ounces) yellow cake mix
    1 can (16 ounces) vanilla pudding
    1 package (11-1/2 ounces) macaroons, crushed
    1 jar (10 ounces) currant jelly
1/2 pint whipping cream
    2 tablespoons sugar
1/2 teaspoon vanilla extract

Bake cake according to package directions, using two 9-in. layer pans. Cool completely. Cut each cake in half horizontally. Combine pudding and macaroons; spread mixture on two layers. Spread jelly on the middle layer and assemble, with a plain layer on top. Whip cream with sugar and vanilla; frost top and sides of cake. Refrigerate until serving. **Yield:** 16-20 servings.

APPLE KUCHEN
Sue Foss, Oregon, Illinois

This simple-to-fix recipe came out of an old Swedish cookbook that my mom always held together with a large rubber band. The recipe is my favorite!

    6 large baking apples, pared and sliced
    2 teaspoons ground cinnamon
    1 cup sugar, *divided*
    1 tablespoon butter
1/2 cup milk
    1 cup all-purpose flour
    1 teaspoon baking powder
VANILLA SAUCE:
    1 cup sugar
    2 tablespoons cornstarch

1/2 teaspoon salt
    2 cups cold water
    2 tablespoons butter
    1 teaspoon vanilla extract

Arrange apples in a 13-in. x 9-in. x 2-in. baking pan. Combine cinnamon and 1/2 cup sugar. Reserve 1 tablespoon; sprinkle remaining mixture over apples. In a mixing bowl, combine butter, milk, remaining sugar, flour and baking powder. Drop by tablespoonfuls over apples; sprinkle reserved cinnamon/sugar on top. Bake at 350° for 35-40 minutes or until golden brown. Meanwhile, for sauce, combine sugar, cornstarch, salt and water in a saucepan. Cook, stirring constantly, over medium heat until thick. Remove from heat; add butter and vanilla. Serve sauce and kuchen warm. **Yield:** 10-12 servings.

QUICK TOFFEE BARS
Jeanette Wubbena, Standish, Michigan

These buttery, beautiful, quick bars are my all-time favorite...and a fast way to fill the cookie jar when company's coming!

    12 graham crackers, broken into quarters
    1 cup butter *or* margarine
1/2 cup sugar
    1 cup chopped nuts
    1 cup (6 ounces) semisweet chocolate chips

Line a 15-in. x 10-in. x 1-in. jelly roll pan with waxed paper and grease the paper. Arrange graham crackers in pan and set aside. In a saucepan, melt butter and sugar over medium heat; let boil gently for 3 minutes. Spread evenly over graham crackers. Sprinkle nuts on top. Bake at 325° for 10 minutes. Cool. Meanwhile, melt chocolate chips; spread over bars and allow to cool again. After chocolate is set, pan can be turned over so waxed paper can be peeled off. Bars can be frozen. **Yield:** 4 dozen.

GRANDMA BUELAH'S APPLE DUMPLINGS
Jenny Hughson, Mitchell, Nebraska

Buelah and Harry Hughson settled in Sioux County, Nebraska in the early 1900's. Grandma had a reputation for being a talented musician, avid card player and a marvelous cook! I always make a double batch of her dumplings for my husband and our four children.

Pastry for double-crust pie
    6 small baking apples, peeled and cored
1/3 cup sugar
    2 tablespoons half-and-half cream
3/4 cup maple *or* maple-flavored syrup, warmed

On a floured surface, roll out pastry to an 18-in. x 12-in. rectangle. Cut into six 6-in. squares. Place an apple on each square. Combine sugar and cream; spoon into each apple center. Moisten edges of pastry; fold up corners to center and pinch to seal. Place on an ungreased 13-in. x 9-in. x 2-in. baking pan. Bake at 450° for 15 minutes. Reduce heat to 350° and continue baking until done, about 30 minutes, basting twice with syrup. Serve warm. **Yield:** 6 servings.

SOUR CREAM COFFEE CAKE
Sandra Munyon, Watertown, Wisconsin

This is a true Wisconsin recipe—using our own delicious sour cream. But, of course, it can be enjoyed anywhere!

        1/2 cup butter, softened
          1 cup sugar
          2 eggs
          1 cup (8 ounces) sour cream
          1 teaspoon vanilla extract
          2 cups all-purpose flour
          1 teaspoon baking powder
          1 teaspoon baking soda
        1/4 teaspoon salt
TOPPING:
        1/4 cup sugar
        1/3 cup packed brown sugar
          2 teaspoons ground cinnamon
        1/2 cup chopped pecans

In a mixing bowl, cream butter and sugar. Add eggs, sour cream and vanilla; mix well. Combine flour, baking powder, soda and salt; add to creamed mixture and beat until combined. Pour half the batter into a greased 13-in. x 9-in. x 2-in. baking pan. Combine topping ingredients; sprinkle half of topping over batter. Add remaining batter and topping. Bake at 325° for 40 minutes or until done. **Yield:** 12-15 servings.

MELTING MOMENTS: Melt chocolate squares for recipes right in their wrappers in the microwave oven. (Be sure the wrappers are paper, *not* foil.) Then just scrape the melted chocolate into the mixing bowl.
  • When melting chocolate in a saucepan, be sure to grease the pan first.
  • When melting chocolate chips for recipes, place in a glass bowl and microwave on low for 1 minute. Stir and microwave 1-2 minutes longer or until melted.

≈♥♥♥≈

EASY CHOCOLATE RICE PUDDING
Wendy Kroeker, Morris, Manitoba

This recipe is the closest I could come to the rice pudding my husband remembers his mother made when he was a boy. I experimented for a long time trying to match that unwritten recipe from the past. Now this is one of my husband's favorite desserts!

          4 cups cold milk
          1 package (3.9 ounces) instant chocolate
            pudding mix
        1/4 cup raisins
        1/4 teaspoon ground cinnamon
          1 cup quick-cooking rice
          1 egg, well beaten
        1/8 teaspoon ground nutmeg

In a medium saucepan, combine all ingredients. Bring to a boil over medium heat. Cool for 5 minutes, stirring twice. Chill until serving. **Yield:** 4 servings.

≈♥♥♥≈

MOON CAKE
Peachy Buffington, West Point, Iowa

I have six grandchildren and this is one of their favorite desserts. If I don't take it to potlucks, I hear lots of groans! Everyone wants the recipe after they've tried it.

CRUST:
          1 cup water
        1/2 cup butter *or* margarine
          1 cup all-purpose flour
          4 eggs
FILLING:
          2 packages (3.4 ounces *each*) instant vanilla
            pudding mix
          3 cups cold milk
          1 package (8 ounces) cream cheese, softened
TOPPING:
          1 carton (8 ounces) frozen whipped topping,
            thawed
Chocolate sauce
Chopped nuts

In a saucepan, bring water and butter to a boil. Add flour all at once and stir until mixture forms a ball. Remove from heat and cool slightly. Add eggs, one at a time, beating well after each addition. Spread on a greased 15-in. x 10-in. x 1-in. jelly roll pan. Bake at 400° for 30 minutes. Cool but do not prick, leaving surface with its "moon-like" appearance. Meanwhile, for filling, beat pudding and milk until thick. Add cream cheese; blend well. Spread on crust; refrigerate 20 minutes. Top with whipped topping. Drizzle chocolate sauce over top and sprinkle with nuts. **Yield:** about 15 servings. **Variation:** Substitute a different flavor of pudding and garnish with chocolate "curls" instead of chocolate sauce.

≈♥♥♥≈

FROZEN CRANBERRY VELVET PIE
Martha Quam, Sioux Falls, South Dakota

This recipe is from my mother's collection. My husband doesn't like pumpkin pie, but he looks forward to this pie at Thanksgiving. It can be made ahead, then served with ease.

          1 package (8 ounces) cream cheese, softened
          1 cup whipping cream
        1/4 cup sugar
        1/2 teaspoon vanilla extract
          1 can (16 ounces) whole cranberry sauce
          1 pie shell (9 inches), baked

In a mixing bowl, beat cream cheese until fluffy. In another bowl, whip whipping cream, sugar and vanilla until thick but not stiff. Add to cream cheese, beating until smooth and creamy. Fold in cranberry sauce. Spoon into pie crust; freeze until firm, at least 4 hours. Remove from freezer 10 minutes before serving. **Yield:** 8-10 servings.

FLAVORFUL FROSTING: Add 1/4 teaspoon flavored gelatin powder to vanilla cake frosting for a pretty color to top off cakes or cupcakes.

DOUBLY DELICIOUS. Thelma's Chocolate Eclair (top) and Velma's Pumpkin Torte (recipes on opposite page).

FROM GRANDMA'S KITCHEN:
Thelma's Chocolate Eclair and Velma's Pumpkin Torte

Velma Gouldie

Thelma Beam

"Our family's sweet tooth goes back at least as far as Grandma's day."

When twin sisters Thelma Beam and Velma Gouldie have each other's families and grandchildren over for dinner, they follow the same rule of thumb they learned long ago from their mother, who learned it from her mother: A meal isn't a meal without dessert!

"We grew up in a large farm family and everyone had a big sweet tooth, so we'd help our mother bake all day on Saturdays," says Thelma (above right), a grandmother of seven from Esbon, Kansas. "She learned how to bake desserts from her mother, and always made sure my brothers had sweets to eat when they'd come in from their chores."

The twins still make many of those down-home desserts they grew up with; in fact, their "taste" in sweets is so similar it sometimes surprises *them*!

"When we don't tell each other what we're going to bring to family reunions or potlucks, we often discover we've brought the *same* thing—two pound cakes or two cherry pies, for instance!" Thelma laughs.

She and her husband, who have five grown sons and a daughter, live just 15 miles from Velma and her husband, who have three grown sons and two grandchildren. They enjoy visiting each other.

They also enjoy sampling and swapping each other's desserts. One popular pie is Velma's Pumpkin Torte—it's a great substitute for pumpkin pie at

Thanksgiving. Another fast favorite is Thelma's Chocolate Eclair. "It's a dessert that our little grandkids love to eat," Thelma says.

The twins' grandchildren not only love eating desserts...they're also showing an early interest in *making* desserts. "Last week, my 4-year-old grandson 'robbed' me of my bowls and spatulas and pretended to fix a batch of cookies!" Velma chuckles.

THELMA'S CHOCOLATE ECLAIR

1/2 box (8 ounces) graham crackers
2 packages (3.4 ounces *each*) instant vanilla pudding mix
3-1/2 cups milk
1 carton (8 ounces) frozen whipped topping, thawed
2 squares (1 ounce *each*) semisweet chocolate
2 tablespoons butter *or* margarine
1 teaspoon light corn syrup
3 tablespoons milk
1 teaspoon vanilla extract
1-1/2 cups sifted confectioners' sugar

Cover the bottom of a 13-in. x 9-in. x 2-in. baking pan with whole graham crackers; set aside. Combine pudding mixes and milk; fold into whipped topping. Spread over graham crackers. Top with another layer of crackers. In a saucepan, melt chocolate and butter. Remove from the heat and add remaining ingredients. Spread over top graham cracker layer. Cover and refrigerate. Dessert is best made 2-3 days ahead of time. **Yield:** 12-15 servings.

VELMA'S PUMPKIN TORTE

CRUST:
1-1/2 cups crushed graham crackers
1/3 cup sugar
1/2 cup butter *or* margarine
FILLING:
2 eggs
3/4 cup sugar
1 package (8 ounces) cream cheese, softened
1 can (16 ounces) pumpkin
3 egg yolks
1/2 cup milk
1/2 cup sugar
1/2 teaspoon salt
1 teaspoon ground cinnamon
1 envelope unflavored gelatin
1/4 cup cold water
1 carton (8 ounces) frozen whipped topping, thawed
Additional whipped topping

Combine crust ingredients; press into the bottom of a 13-in. x 9-in. x 2-in. baking pan. In a mixing bowl, combine eggs, sugar and cream cheese. Beat until smooth. Spread over crust. Bake at 350° for 20-25 minutes or until top appears set. Cool. Meanwhile, combine pumpkin, egg yolks, milk, sugar, salt and cinnamon in a saucepan. Cook, stirring constantly, until mixture thickens; remove from heat. Dissolve gelatin in water; add to saucepan. Fold in whipped topping. Spread over cooled torte; chill. Serve with a dollop of whipped topping. Torte keeps well for several days in the refrigerator. **Yield:** 12-15 servings.

Old-Time Recipe Yielded New Family Favorite

I was born and raised on a farm in North Carolina and learned to cook from the best teachers—my mother and both grandmothers and great-grandmothers! Then I married a farmer who had a few of his own grandmother's recipes up his sleeve.

I found out about one as I was preparing to make a big, traditional, chocolate-frosted layer cake for my husband's birthday. Instead he handed me a recipe he enjoyed as a boy called Biscuit & Applesauce Cake, which consists of leftover biscuits covered with sweetened applesauce. Well, you can imagine my surprise!

The recipe originated with his grandmother, who had 13 children to feed and knew how to *stretch* everything! She would prepare Biscuit & Applesauce Cake often as a treat for her grandchildren.

I obliged and made the "cake" for my husband —decorating it with birthday candles—and to my surprise (again!), it was a huge hit! This dessert is a welcome change from cakes loaded with icing, and it couldn't be simpler. The measurements aren't precise, but it seems most country cooks did their finest cooking with bits and pinches and dashes of this and that. Try this recipe and see for yourself.

INGREDIENTS: **Leftover biscuits, split in half**
Applesauce
Sugar *(Yes, that's all!)*

Heat the applesauce and sweeten with sugar to taste. In a large bowl, layer biscuits and applesauce, ending with applesauce. Cover completely with the sauce. Cover the bowl and chill. Serve at room temperature.
—*Derona Williams*
Candler, North Carolina

TWO-MINUTE COOKIES
Kerry Bouchard, Shawmut, Montana

My mom used to pack these cookies into our school lunches. They're inexpensive and easy to prepare, so all seven of us children learned to make them. Now they're also a favorite of my two children's.

   1/2 cup butter *or* margarine
   1/2 cup milk
   2 cups sugar
   3 cups quick-cooking *or* rolled oats
   5 tablespoons unsweetened cocoa
   1/2 cup raisins, chopped nuts *or* coconut

In a large saucepan, heat butter, milk and sugar. Bring to a boil, stirring occasionally. Boil for 1 minute. Remove from the heat. Stir in oats, cocoa and raisins, nuts or coconut. Drop by tablespoonfuls onto waxed paper. Cool. **Yield:** about 3 dozen.

CHOCOLATE WHIPPED CREAM CAKE
Ruth Shelliam, Spring Green, Wisconsin

Chocolate fans will love this double chocolate dessert cake!

   1 box (18-1/4 ounces) chocolate cake mix
   1 pint whipping cream *or* 1 carton (8 ounces) frozen whipped topping, thawed
   1/3 cup sugar
   1/4 cup unsweetened cocoa

Prepare cake mix according to package directions, using two 9-in. round cake pans. Cool completely after baking. If using whipping cream, place it in a chilled mixing bowl; beat, gradually adding sugar and cocoa, until stiff peaks form. If using whipped topping, place in a bowl and fold in sugar and cocoa. Frost one cake layer with whipped cream mixture; top with second layer and frost entire cake. Refrigerate 24 hours before serving. **Yield:** 16-20 servings.

> **DUST WITH COCOA:** When baking a chocolate cake, dust your baking pans with unsweetened cocoa instead of flour to avoid that white "floury" look.

STRAWBERRY BAVARIAN TORTE
Christine Azzarello, Elmhurst, Illinois

This beautiful make-ahead dessert is deliciously light... the perfect ending to any meal.

   1 package (6 ounces) strawberry-flavored gelatin
   1 cup boiling water
   2 quarts fresh strawberries, sliced
   1/2 pint heavy cream, whipped
   1 sponge cake, cut into cubes
Additional whipped cream
Whole strawberries for garnish

In a bowl, dissolve gelatin in water. Add berries; allow to thicken partially. Fold in whipped cream. Fold in cake cubes; stir until well coated. Spread into a greased springform pan; cover and chill overnight. Remove from pan and place on a torte plate. Frost with whipped cream and garnish with berries. **Yield:** 10-12 servings.

PUMPKIN PUDDING
Abby Albrecht, Clarence, New York

I love pumpkin, and this recipe—given to me by my mother —takes only minutes to make! I consider it a harvest pudding...perfect for the fall and the holidays.

   1 cup solid-pack pumpkin
   1 tablespoon molasses
   1/2 teaspoon ground cinnamon
   1/8 teaspoon ground cloves
   1/4 teaspoon salt
1-1/2 cups cold milk

1 package (3.4 ounces) instant vanilla
    pudding mix
1/2 cup whipping cream, whipped
Additional whipped cream, optional
Additional ground cinnamon, optional

In a mixing bowl, combine pumpkin, molasses and spices. Gradually add milk. Add pudding mix; beat slowly with an electric mixer until thick, about 1 minute. Fold in whipped cream. Pour into a serving bowl or individual serving dishes. Chill for 1 hour. If desired, top each serving with a dollop of whipped cream and a sprinkle of cinnamon. **Yield:** 9-12 servings.

QUICK GRAHAM CRACKER CAKE
Mary Lou McCullough, New Galilee, Pennsylvania

Imagine two food favorites—graham crackers and whipped cream—in one wonderful cake. The results are heavenly!

1-1/4 cups graham cracker crumbs, *divided*
    1 box (18-1/4 ounces) white cake mix
    2 tablespoons sugar
1-1/2 cups water
    2 egg whites
    4 tablespoons vegetable oil
    1 pint whipping cream, whipped *or* 1 carton
    (12 ounces) frozen whipped topping,
    thawed

Set aside 2 tablespoons graham cracker crumbs. Place remaining crumbs, cake mix, sugar, water, egg whites and oil in a large mixing bowl. Beat for 2 minutes. Pour into two greased and floured 9-in. layer pans. Bake at 350° for 25-30 minutes. Let stand a few minutes before removing from pans. Cool completely on a wire rack, then split each cake in half horizontally. Spread whipped cream between layers and frost entire cake. Sprinkle reserved graham cracker crumbs on top. Refrigerate until serving time. **Yield:** 16-20 servings.

CHOCOLATE DREAM DESSERT
Delores Searls, Atwood, Kansas

I've been married 37 years and have four grandchildren, and this is our all-time favorite dessert. Its chocolate flavor is subtle but delicious. The last time I made it, my brother said, "This has got to be the best dessert there is!" See if you agree!

CRUST:
    1 cup all-purpose flour
    1/2 cup butter *or* margarine
    1 cup pecans, finely chopped
FILLING:
    1 package (8 ounces) cream cheese, softened
    1 cup confectioners' sugar
    1 carton (8 ounces) frozen whipped topping,
    thawed, *divided*
    1 package (3.4 ounces) instant vanilla
    pudding mix
    1 package (3.9 ounces) instant chocolate
    pudding mix
    3 cups cold milk
    1 chocolate bar, grated

Combine crust ingredients until crumb-like; press into the bottom of a 13-in. x 9-in. x 2-in. baking pan. Bake at 350° for 15-20 minutes or until golden brown. Cool. Place cream cheese, sugar and half the whipped topping in a mixing bowl; whip until smooth. Spread over crust. Prepare pudding mixes with milk; mix until smooth and thickened. Spread over cream cheese mixture; chill until firm. Spread remaining whipped topping on top, then sprinkle grated chocolate over topping. Refrigerate until serving. **Yield:** 12-15 servings.

LEMONADE PIE
Peggy Fine, Helena, Montana

The tangy taste of this pie makes it a hit in the summertime. (We especially like it after a spicy meal.) I love making desserts, and whenever we have a potluck at church, everybody knows I'll be bringing a dessert.

    1 can (14 ounces) sweetened condensed milk
    1 can (12 ounces) frozen pink lemonade,
    thawed and undiluted
    1 carton (6 ounces) frozen whipped topping,
    thawed
    1 graham cracker crust (9 inches)
Graham cracker crumbs

In a bowl, combine milk, lemonade and whipped topping. Pour into the crust. Refrigerate for at least 12 hours. Garnish with graham cracker crumbs. **Yield:** 8 servings.

NUTTY NEWS: Toasting nuts brings out their flavor and aroma. Spread whole or chopped nuts on a cookie sheet in a single layer and bake at 350° until lightly browned, about 5 minutes. Watch carefully.

BANANA WALNUT CAKE
Sherry Reynolds, Orelana, Pennsylvania

I like to serve this cake for family birthdays. It's everyone's favorite, and you can freeze it ahead...it's tastier with age!

    1 box (18-1/4 ounces) banana cake mix
    3/4 teaspoon baking powder
    3 medium bananas
    3 eggs
    1/2 cup water
    1/3 cup vegetable oil
1-1/2 cups chopped walnuts
CRUMB TOPPING:
    1/2 cup sugar
    1/2 cup all-purpose flour
    1/4 cup butter

Place first seven ingredients in a large mixing bowl. Beat on low speed just until combined, then on medium for 2 minutes. Pour into a greased and floured 10-in. tube pan or a 13-in. x 9-in. x 2-in. baking pan. In a small bowl, combine topping ingredients until crumbly; sprinkle evenly over batter. Bake at 350° for 45 minutes. Cool. Store well-wrapped in refrigerator. **Yield:** 16-20 servings.

♥ INDEX ♥

KITCHEN HELP

❤ Before You Begin Baking, 6
❤ Simplified Weights and Measures, 30
❤ Ingredient Substitutions, 81

TO ORDER additional copies of this book, specify Code 7429 and send $10.98 each plus $2.50 for postage and handling to: Country Store, Suite 3088, P.O. Box 612, Milwaukee WI 53201. Credit card customers (Discover, Master Card, Visa and American Express) can phone **toll-free 1-800/ 558-1013** from 7 a.m. to 9 p.m. (Central Time) Monday-Friday and 8 a.m. to 3:30 p.m. on Saturdays.